STORY SPARKLERS

(Starters and Extenders for
66 Noted Children's Picture Books)

By

Jean Stangl

Cover Illustration By
Anita C. Nelson

Inside Illustrations By
Liza Sernett

Publishers
T.S. Denison & Co., Inc.
Minneapolis, Minnesota 55431

Dedication

For Lee Ann

Standard Book Number: 513-02054-3
Story Sparklers
Copyright © 1991 by the T.S. Denison & Co., Inc.
Minneapolis, Minnesota 55431

Part I – INTRODUCTION

Story Sparklers contains an overview of sixty-six favorite picture books along with sparkling ideas to be used to introduce and extend picture books and oral storytelling. By using this book, teachers, parents, librarians, and other storytellers will discover that storytime is more than just reading a book. These innovative story book starters will introduce the story, set the mood, and capture the attention of your audience.

After reading the book, involve your audience by using these fun-filled activities and projects to extend the story idea into all areas of the curriculum.

These easy to prepare literature based activities which include patterns, Fun Sheets and a list of easy to obtain materials, will take your young audience *into* the book through the pre-activities, *through* the book as it is read, and then *beyond* the book through the reinforcement activities.

The wide variety of projects give young children extensive opportunities to exercise their creative abilities and logical thinking skills. Children should be allowed and encouraged to become as actively involved as possible in "doing" as much of the preparation and procedure as they are capable of.

Although books are listed under a specific topic heading, they easily cross over and can be used under other categories.

Part II – STARTERS

There are numerous ways to introduce books to a young audience, but the story starters you find here are especially developed for each book. By first using these mood setters that focus on key parts of the story, you will capitalize on the natural curiosity of young children as they eagerly await the reading of the book.

Related finger plays, nursery rhymes and poems, as well as songs, games and riddles, are good "attention getters." You will also discover how live animals and insects, plants, seeds and other nature items can become effective visual aids for introducing a child's favorite picture book. Sensory awareness and science experiments add hands-on experiences that relate to the story book.

Part III EXTENDERS

Extend the learning possibilities of the book by stretching your storytelling time into story related activities that will reinforce the story idea, provide take-home projects, stimulate imagination and creativity and involve youngsters in classroom cooperative experiences.

Concept discovery, creative movement and dramatic play are just a few of the fun activities that will help reinforce information presented in the story. Creative art activities and projects, puppetry and the Fun Sheets all provide tangible means for story recall.

Table of Contents

Chapter 1
TINY CREATURES

Insects and spiders can be collected and safely kept one to two days in the classroom. They should then be returned to their natural environment. A plastic peanut butter jar makes a safe, easy-to-view container. Add a small tree branch, pebbles and a few leaves to the jar. Spray the leaves lightly to provide moisture and water for the insects. Cover the top with fine net mesh and secure with a strong rubber band. Keep the jar away from the sun. Provide magnifying glasses.

The Picture Books

Book 1   *The Biggest House In The World*, Leo Lionni

Book 2   *The Grouchy Ladybug*, Eric Carle

Book 3   *The Honeybee And The Robber*, Eric Carle

Book 4   *The Hungry Caterpillar*, Eric Carle

Book 5   *Inch By Inch*, Leo Lionni

Book 6   *The Very Busy Spider*, Eric Carle

THE BIGGEST HOUSE IN THE WORLD

Leo Lionni

(Pantheon, 1968)

Upon declaring he wants to grow the biggest shell house in the world, the wise father tells the little snail a story that convinces him a little house is what he really wants.

STARTERS

Garden snails are easy to find in early morning in damp places or under rocks or logs. Bring them to the classroom in your collection jar. Snails are fascinating creatures. Garden snails have over 25,000 tiny saw-like teeth, no legs, crawl on their stomach foot, and can live two to three years without eating. Their eyes are the knobs located on the ends of the longest tentacles (feelers). One of nature's scavengers, they can be kept for several days in a snailery.

Materials Needed:

1. Empty aquarium, soft, moist soil, decaying leaves, water spray bottle, magnifying glasses.

2. Wax paper, 3 x 5 cards cut in half, ink stamp pad.

Procedure:

1. Prepare the snailery by adding about 4 inches of moist soil to the aquarium. Place piles of dead leaves in the corners. Mist soil, leaves and sides of aquarium. Add several lively snails. Mist as needed to keep area moist but never spray the snails.

2. Set the snails on the paper; locate stomach, tentacles, eyes and tail.

   Can you find two shells with exact patterns. Have children make their thumb print on a card. Compare. Each snail shell has a different pattern just as each thumb print is different.

3. Have children contribute to a list of words that rhyme with snail (there are over 60).

EXTENDERS

Materials Needed:
1. Patterns from page 11 (large pail, nail, snail tail, rail, mail, whale), contact paper, scissors.

2. Tempera paint, flat pans, white paper.

Procedure:
1. Check children's observation by asking the number of tentacles, where the eyes are located, and how the snail moves. Can you find a silvery trail made by the snails? Which side of the shell is the spiral on?

2. For a seriation activity, set the snails on the wax paper and have children help put them in order smallest to largest just as the little snail's shell grew. Have children gather like items in different sizes – blocks, spools, toy cars. Seriate from small to large and then from large to small.

3. Trace and cut patterns using tag board. Cover with clear contact paper. Set up the patterns on the floor to form an obstacle course. Give directions for walking around the pail, over the nail, between the mail and whale, and so on. Children can take turns arranging the patterns and giving directions.

4. Add different color paint to each pan until just the bottom of the pan is covered. Allow the snail to move about and then place it on the paper and let it make a snail-trail design. Tempera paint is nontoxic and will not harm the snails. After the project, place the snails in a shallow pan of water for a few seconds and then return the snails to their natural habitat.

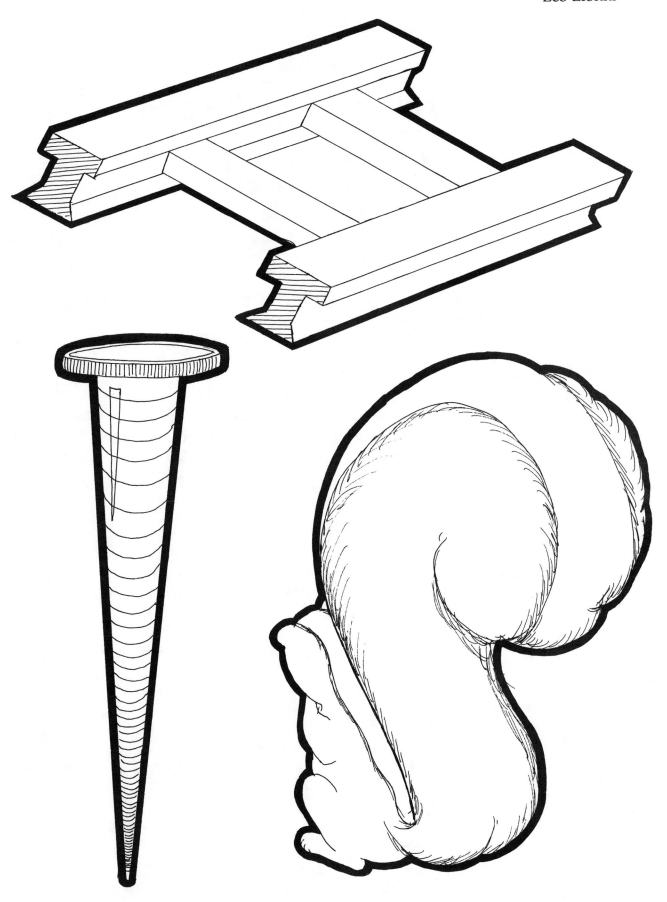

THE GROUCHY LADYBUG

Eric Carle

(Crowell, 1977)

Grouchy ladybug's friends help her discover that it is better to be happy and have friends then to be grouchy.

STARTERS

Observe ladybugs either outdoors or viewed through a jar in the classroom. Ladybugs help the environment by eating aphids and cotton scale that attacks citrus trees, roses, and other plants. One ladybug will eat over a 1,000 harmful insects in its short life time.

Materials Needed:
   Live ladybugs in a jar.

Procedure:

1. Recite the rhyme, "Ladybug, Ladybug," and then have the children join-in as you repeat it.

2. Questions: Can a ladybug fly? Where are its wings? Observe the ladybug as it unfolds its wings, flies and refolds the wings.

   The ladybug in this story book was grouchy. Do you ever feel grouchy? Why? Show me how your face would look if your were feeling grouchy.

3. Count the spots on the ladybugs. Some ladybugs have 3, 5, 7, 21 or none at all.

EXTENDERS

Materials Needed:

1. Stick puppet – orange construction paper, felt markers, tongue depressor sticks, glue, scissors.

2. Finger puppet – a cup cut from a cardboard egg carton, felt markers, rubber band.

Procedure.

1. For each puppet cut two circles from construction paper. Make a happy face on one circle and a grouchy face on the other. Glue one face to each side of the top of the stick (back to back). Let the children take turns showing their grouchy face puppet and sharing one thing that makes them feel grouchy. Do the same with the happy face puppet.

2. Use the markers to add dots and features to the egg cup, Place a rubber band over the top of the cup and slip your finger between the rubber band and the underneath side of the cup. Use the finger puppet to dramatize the Ladybug rhyme.

Book 3

THE HONEYBEE AND THE ROBBER

Eric Carle

(Philomel, 1981)

The life cycle of bees told in story form with surprise tabs. The honeybee overcomes the robber (bear) by stinging it on the nose.

STARTERS

Materials Needed:
1. Flowers, jar of honey containing honeycomb, crackers, spoons. Optional: empty honeycombs, check with a beekeeper or a supply store.

Procedure:
1. If possible observe bees buzzing in flowers and listen for their sounds. Show the cover of the book and discuss the three body parts, 6 legs and other features. Bees pick up pollen on the hairs on their legs. The tongue is a flexible tube that sucks water, nectar and honey into the bee's mouth.

2. Examine flowers pointing out the pollen and sticky nectar. Spoon the honey onto the crackers. Discuss smell, taste and texture. Who do you think eats honey? (bears, ants, flies, people). Where do you think bees live?

3. Children can recite this "buzzing bee" rhyme while using their fingers for counting.

> One little honeybee buzzing all around.
> Two little honeybees buzzing up and down.
> Three little honeybees buzzing off to town.
> Four little honeybees buzzing on a mound.
> Five little honeybees make a buzzing sound.
> Buzzzzz, buzzzzz, buzzzzz, buzzzzz, buzzzzz.

EXTENDERS

Materials Needed:
1. Fun Sheet on page 18, crayons.

2. Fun Sheet on page 19, scissors, crayons, glue, and sheets of yellow construction paper.

3. Assorted sets of building blocks.

Procedure:
1. Make copies of the Fun Sheet for each child.

2. Give each child a copy of the Fun Sheet, scissors and a piece of yellow paper. Have them cut out and then assemble the parts of the bee onto the yellow paper. Glue in place. Draw in the legs and other features.

3. Form small groups and have each group use blocks to build a home for bees. Tell why the bees would like your house.

Directions: Draw a line from the bee to its home in our story.

- -

Directions: Circle the robber in our story. Color all the pictures.

Book 4

THE HUNGRY CATERPILLAR

Eric Carle

(World, 1969)

The life cycle of a butterfly. Interesting foods are used for counting. Days of the week, day and night, and other concepts are cleverly presented as caterpillar eats his fill.

STARTERS

Materials Needed:

1. Live caterpillar, pupa, and a butterfly or any one stage, pictures (*World Book Encyclopedia* is a good source), or a chart showing the four stages.

2. Pictures of butterflies and moths.

3. Large box of crayons.

4. Long green balloon, black felt marking pen.

Procedure:

1. Explain the four stages of the butterfly (egg, pupa or chrysalis larva or caterpillar and adult butterfly). Discuss the differences in size, shape and color.

2. Find a picture of the butterfly that matches the color of the one in the jar.

3. From the pictures, have children take turns finding a butterfly color, and then removing the matching crayon from the box to discover how many different colors can be found in butterflies.

4. Inflate the balloon slightly, pause, continue to blow in air, pausing several times to ask what is happening to the balloon. Set the balloon aside.

EXTENDERS

Repeat the above balloon activity relating it to the caterpillar in the story. Ask what made the balloon grow larger and what made the caterpillar grow. Tie the end of the inflated balloon, and use a black felt marker to draw eyes and antennae.

Materials Needed:
1. Playdough, paint, brushes.

2. White paper, paint and small brushes.

3. Old crayons, hand pencil sharpeners, wax paper, scissors, tape, butterfly pattern on page 22.

4. Colored cup cake papers, large paper clips, string, small tree branches.

Procedure:
1. Form the first three stages of the butterfly from playdough. Set in the sun to harden and then paint.

2. Paint your own butterfly on paper.

3. Butterfly – grate old crayons and sprinkle several colors on one piece of wax paper. Place the second sheet of paper on top and carefully set the project in the sun. When the crayon shavings are melted, bring inside to cool. Trace the butterfly pattern onto the wax paper with a felt marker and cut out. Tape the butterflies to a sunny window (or tape a string to the back for taking home).

4. Mobile – flatten and decorate three cup cake papers with crayons or felt markers. Gather each paper at the center and secure the gathers with a paper clip. Fan out the wings. Tie different lengths of string to each paper clip. Tie the other ends of the strings to the tree branch. Add a loop of string for hanging the mobile.

Book 5

INCH BY INCH

Leo Lionni

(Scholastic, 1960)

An inchworm outsmarts a robin by showing her how he can measure her and the other birds in the woods.

STARTERS

If you see tiny round holes in a leaf, look on the underneath side and you may find a tiny inchworm.

Materials Needed:
Large leaf cut from green paper, piece of green yarn, hole punch, glue.

Procedure:
Prepare a leaf ahead of time by punching out a few holes and gluing a tiny piece of yarn (worm) on the underneath side. Show the leaf and ask what would make holes like these in a leaf. After several suggestions, turn the leaf over and show the inchworm.

Show the live inchworm if you have one. Observe how it moves. It has legs only on the front and back of its body and it humps the middle of it body by pulling the rear part close to the front part. Then it pushes the front part of its body forward to its full length and starts the process again.

EXTENDERS

Materials Needed:

1. Paper leaves, hole punch, green yarn, glue.

2. Yarn cut into lengths as follows – red, one foot; yellow, two feet; blue, three feet, classroom chart, felt markers.

Procedure:

1. Have each child make their own inchworms and leaf as above.

2. Show children how to use the yarn to measure objects in the classroom (this will not be accurate but it will provide an introduction to measurements). After experimenting with the measuring yarn, assign each child to measure an object – table, wall, floor. Record the measurements on a class chart (table – 2 blue and 1 red = 7 feet).

3. Creative movement: Pretend you are an inchworm. Review how the inchworm moved by humping its back – **hump, pull** (legs in), **push** (arms out in front), **stretch** and repeat. Give directions for the inchworms to move slowly to the wall; move fast; move backward; move in circles. Let children take turns giving directions.

Book 6

THE VERY BUSY SPIDER

Eric Carle

(Philomel, 1984)

As spider starts to build a web, various farm animals come along asking the spider to join them in some fun. But spider is too busy building her web. Children can both see and feel the textured web as it grows in size.

STARTERS

Observe and discuss the live spider. A spider is not an insect. A spider has two body sections and eight legs; insects have three body sections and six legs. Introduce the story by reciting the rhyme, *Little Miss Muffet*. Sing the *Eeensy Weensy Spider* song with actions.

Materials Needed:
Spider web collection – several sheets of black construction paper, clear plastic folder covers.

Procedure:
Locate spider webs (early in the morning is the best time). Place a sheet of black paper behind the web and quickly pull it forward against the web. The web will stick to the paper. Collect as many as possible. Place between plastic folder covers. Discuss shapes and sizes and how a web is made (from the spinnerets located in the rear of the abdomen).

EXTENDERS

Materials Needed:

1. Black construction paper, white liquid glue in squeeze bottle, small spider cut from felt.

2. Black construction paper, black yarn, newspapers torn into tiny pieces, stapler, scissors, pattern on page 27.

Procedure:

1. Squeeze the white glue onto the paper to form a web design. Let dry and then glue a felt spider to the web.

2. Use the pattern to cut two large spiders from black construction paper. Staple the two together leaving a small open space. Stuff the body section only with torn paper, and finish stapling. Cut eight strips of black paper and accordion pleat each. Staple legs to the front section of the spider. Staple a length of yarn to the top of the spider to use in making the spider walk and bounce.

3. Pretend you are a spider (have children get on hands and knees). Show me how you would move to spin a big square web; a circle web, a rectangle web, a triangle web.

4. You and your spider jump together around the table; hop to the door; walk backwards. Let children take turns giving directions.

Chapter 2
GROWING THINGS

Planting quick growing seeds and rooting cuttings in water will help children understand the growth cycle as well as provide a reinforcement for the story's theme. After cuttings have developed a good root system and seedlings have several leaves, they can be transferred to pots or set outside in the garden. Plants should be kept moist but not over watered. Most plants require some sun.

The Picture Books

Book 1   *The Carrot Seed*, Ruth Krauss

Book 2   *Growing Vegetable Soup*, Lois Ehlert

Book 3   *Jelly Glass Farm*, Kathy Mandry

Book 4   *Rosa's Special Garden*, Dale Fife

Book 5   *The Tiny Seed*, Eric Carle

Book 6   *A Tree Is Nice*, Janice Udrey

THE CARROT SEED
Ruth Krauss
(Harper, 1966)

A little boy is determined to grow a carrot from seed despite the negative outlook of each family member.

STARTERS

Materials Needed:
> Bunch of carrots with tops, package of carrot seeds.

Procedure:
> Examine the carrots. Discuss color, texture and the part that grows underground. Carrots are root vegetables. Can you think of other root vegetables?

> Sing *Here We Go Arround the Mulberry Bush*, substituting:

> This is the way we plant our seeds.
> This is the way we water our seeds.
> This is the way the sun shines on our seeds.
> This is the way our carrot seeds grows.

> Let children do their own action as they sing.

EXTENDERS

Materials Needed:
> 1. Large carrots, peanut butter, serrated plastic knives, napkins.
>
> 2. Clean margarine tubs, large flower pot, potting soil, old spoons.
>
> 3. Carrot pattern, page 33, scissors crayons, paper.

Procedure:

1. Cut tops from carrots leaving a one-inch piece of the carrot. Wash and slice the carrots into wheel shapes. Spread peanut butter on one wheel and top with a second one to make a carrot sandwich. Compare the color, texture and tastes of the carrot and the peanut butter.

2. Cut the tops from the one-inch pieces leaving a tiny bit of green. Place in the margarine tubs and add enough water to cover half the carrot. New green shoots should appear in three or four days.

   Fill the flower pots with potting soil and plant the carrot seeds according to the directions on the package. Compare the growth of the two "gardens." Will the top and the seed both produce carrots?

3. Give each child a copy of the carrot to color. Cut a slit five inches long across the center of the sheet of paper. Below the slit draw a seed with roots. Place the carrot into the slit behind the paper. Sing the song above and watch the carrot grow as you slowly push it up. "Pull" the carrot from the ground.

Book 2

GROWING VEGETABLE SOUP

Lois Ehlert

(Harcourt, 1987)

Story tells the cycle of seeds – prepare the garden, plant vegetable seeds, water, wait, watch it grow, pick it, prepare it, and make vegetable soup.

STARTERS

Materials Needed:
Large grocery bag, variety of fresh vegetables.

Procedure:
Ask children to name some vegetables. Set out the vegetables. Sort them by color, then by size. Find the largest and the smallest. Place them in order largest to smallest.

Place the vegetables in the bag and have each child reach in and identify one vegetable by feeling it.

EXTENDERS

Materials Needed:
1. Electric skillet, plastic serrated knives, cutting boards, water, wooden spoon, ladle, spoons and bowls or cups. Salt and pepper are optional.

2. Patterns from page 36, red, orange, light brown and green construction paper, plastic drinking straws, stapler, felt markers.

Procedure:

1. Wash, pare only if necessary, cut into bite-size pieces and place in the skillet. Add one cup of water to each cup of vegetables. Cook until tender but still crisp. Stir frequently. Ladle into cups and eat! Requires constant adult supervision.

2. Make copies of the vegetables on appropriate colored paper. Each child selects a vegetable, cuts it out and draws on a happy face. Staple the vegetable to the top of a straw to make a puppet.

   Have children sit on the floor holding their puppet. Give directions by chanting:

   > Carrot stand up
   > Tomato stand up
   > Potato and cabbage stand up, stand up
   > Tomato sit down
   > Potato sit down
   > Cabbage and carrot sit down, sit down

   Repeat substituting the color for vegetable (red stand up).

tomato

carrot

potato

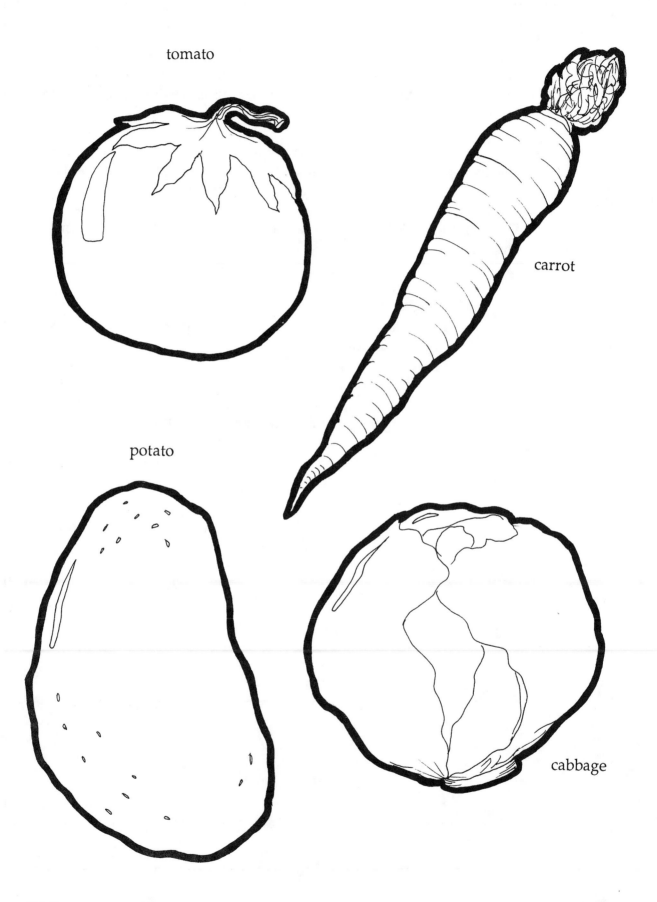

cabbage

Book 3

JELLY GLASS FARM
Kathy Mandry
(Pantheon, 1974)

A child grows a garden in jelly glasses, pans, bowls, and an old "sneaker."

STARTERS

Materials Needed:
1. Orange, pineapple, avocado, sweet potato, and 4 medium size paper bags.

2. Four-inch cuttings from house plants such as Coleus, Creeping Charlie, Wandering Jew, Philodendron.

Procedure:
1. Place one item in each bag. Divide the class into groups of 2 or 3. Give each group a bag and allow a few minutes for them to decide on ways to describe the vegetable. Each member of the group gives a clue and the other class members try to guess what it is.

2. Set out the cuttings and ask if children have any of these plants at home. Identify by name. Compare the leaves, textures, and colors.

EXTENDERS

Materials Needed:
1. Orange, pineapple, avocado and sweet potato from above, flower pot filled with potting soil, pie pan, clear plastic cup and 2 toothpicks, bowl, water, serrated plastic picnic knives.

2. Cuttings from above, clear plastic drinking cups, water.

3. Sunflower and grass seed, pair of old sneakers, potting soil, old spoons, water.

Procedure:

1. Cut the orange into small pieces and remove seeds. Let them dry. Plant 1-inch deep in the pot of soil. Water and place in a sunny window.

   Cut the top from the pineapple leaving 2-inches of the meat. Set the top in the pan. Add water to cover the pineapple part. Set in a sunny window.

   Cut the avocado and remove the seed. Push toothpick into the center of the seed on opposite sides. Suspend it over a glass of water with the pointed end up. Place it in a dark area until roots and a green shoot appear. Move to a sunny window.

   Cut the sweet potato in half lengthwise. Place one half, cut side down, in the bowl (save the other half for tasting). Add water to cover one-third of the sweet potato. Place in an area with good light.

   Compare the plants to those in the story.

   Peel, cut into bit-size pieces and sample each fruit.

2. Explain that these cuttings will root and grow in water. Place each type cutting in half glass of water. Roots should appear in four to five days.

3. Punch holes in the bottom of the sneakers. Fill with potting soil. Plant grass in one; sunflowers in the other. Place in a sunny spot and keep moist. Observe for the first two or three days or until they note any changes. Give each child a Fun Sheet found on page 39 and crayons and each day, for the next five days, illustrate the growth in each sneaker.

	Grass Seeds					Sunflower Seeds			
5	4	3	2	1	5	4	3	2	1

Book 4

ROSA'S SPECIAL GARDEN

Dale Fife
(Whitman, 1985)

Each member of four-year old Rosa's family has a garden plot. They all tell Rosa she is too little to grow a garden.

Rosa claims a bare spot of ground and entertains a visiting bird, dog, and cat. Her "garden" is so special that even her family comes to visit.

STARTERS

Materials Needed:
1. Seed catalogs, or fruit, vegetable, and flower pictures from the advertising section of newspaper.

Procedure:
1. Ask who has a garden? Who takes care of it? What do you grow? Discuss things that grow.

2. Cut the pictures into squares and lay out on the floor. Decide which ones grow under the ground, on trees, vines and bushes, and sort into piles. Help children identify each.

EXTENDERS

Materials Needed:
1. Paper, crayons.

2. Large sheet of butcher paper, felt markers, scissors, glue, pictures from above.

3. Several feet of colored yarn, stuffed animals, puppets, dolls.

Procedure:
1. If you had a special garden, what would you have in it? Give each child paper and crayons to draw their special garden.

2. To make a class mural, draw a brown wavy line across the bottom third of the paper. Outline a tree, bush and vines. Cut out the food and flower pictures and glue to the mural to show where each grows.

3. Decide on a special place (indoors or outdoors) to be our special garden. Mark the boundary with yarn. Have each child select a "friend" to bring to the garden. Read the story again.

Book 5

THE TINY SEED
Eric Carle
(Picture Book Studios, 1987)

Cycle of the seed through the seasons. The wind blows the tiny seed over the mountain, desert and sea until it falls to earth where it sprouts, grows, blooms, goes to seed and is again carried off by the wind.

STARTERS

Materials Needed:

1. Fast-growing seeds – grass, popcorn, radish, lima bean, bowl of water.

2. Seed pods from weeds, flowers, trees, grasses.

Procedure:

1. Examine the seeds and compare, size, shape and color.

2. Soak 3 lima beans in bowl of water until after the story.

3. Break open the seed pods. How are they alike? Different?

   If possible let children blow dandelion or milkweed seed pods and observe how the are carried by the wind in tiny parachutes (tiny bits of cotton could also be used).

EXTENDERS

Materials Needed:

1. The lima beans soaked in water from above, magnifying glasses.

2. Bottom of egg cartons cut into four cup sections, seeds from above, cotton balls, medicine droppers, water.

3. Fun Sheet from page 44, scissors, glue.

Procedure:

1. Split the lima beans in half to show the baby plant inside. Point out leaf and roots. Explain that inside each seed is a baby plant.

2. Give each child a 4-cup egg section. Put three cotton balls in each cup. Use the medicine dropper to wet the cotton thoroughly. Place seeds on top of the moist cotton, one type to each cup. Set in a warm place. When green sprouts appear, place in the sun. Keep the cotton wet. Should sprout in two to four days.

3. Review what happened to the tiny seed in the story. Give each child a Fun Sheet. Have them cut off the strip of pictures, cut the pictures apart, and glue in the order of "The Tiny Seed."

A TREE IS NICE

Janice Udrey

(Harper, 1956)

Trees fill up the sky, grow by the river, give shade, have branches for climbing and hanging a swing, and are nice to picnic under. Some bear fruit and drop their leaves.

STARTERS

Materials Needed:
1. Paper bag.

2. Individual snack bags containing trail mix.

Procedure:
1. Take a silent (no talking) walk around the block or in the yard to look at trees. Sit down under a tree and discuss size, colors, leaf shapes. Look for the tallest tree; smallest tree. What do you like about trees? Compare how it feels sitting in the sun with sitting in the shade of the tree.

   Hug a tree. How does it feel? Do your arms reach around it?

2. Have children help collect items related to trees – bark, large leaf, piece of wood, newspaper, pine cone, twig, small bag of sawdust, toothpaste box. Discuss uses for trees and the importance of caring for trees.

   Secretly place one item at a time in a bag and let children feel and identify.

3. Read the book while sitting under a tree and then pass out snack bags and have a picnic.

EXTENDERS

Materials Need:

1. Flat pieces of bark, paper, broken crayons with paper removed.

2. Assorted leaves, paint and brushes, large sheets of white paper.

3. Red, green, orange and brown sheets of construction paper, scissors, paper fasteners (brads), felt markers, leaf pattern from page 47.

Procedure:

1. Place a sheet of paper over a piece of bark. Rub over the bark with the side of a crayon for a bark rubbing print.

2. Paint one side of a leaf. Press the paint side down on a piece of paper, rub gently and remove for a leaf print.

3. Use the pattern to cut 4 leaves each a different color. Hold the leaves by the stems, overlap each to form a fan. Fasten the fan with a paper fastener (brad) so the fan will open and fold. Write one word of the book title, *A Tree Is Nice*, on each leaf so it can be read as the fan unfolds.

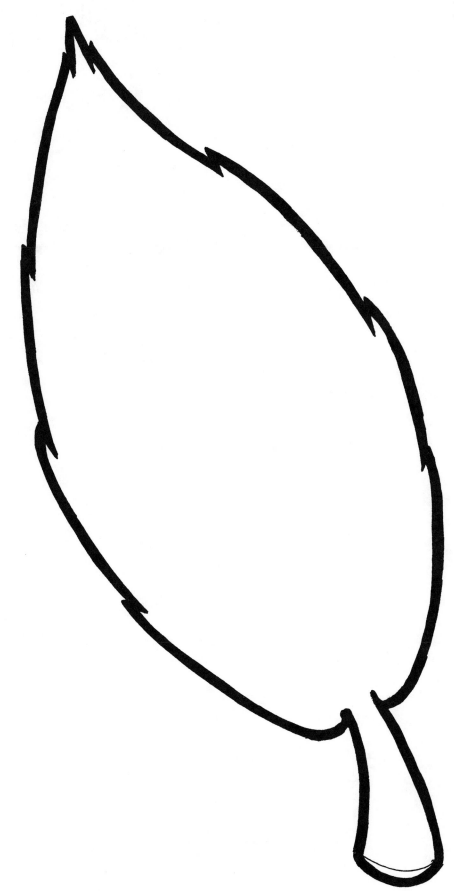

Chapter 3

WEATHER AND SEASONS

No matter where you live, these picture books will help children understand the changes in the weather and the seasons, the importance of these changes, and will introduce them to new experiences.

The Picture Books

Book 1   *Where Does The Sun Go At Night?*, Mirra Ginsburg

Book 2   *Gilberto And The Wind*, Marie Hall Ets

Book 3   *It Looks Like Spilt Milk*, Charles Shaw

Book 4   *Mushroom In The Rain*, Mirra Ginsburg

Book 5   *Rain Makes Applesauce*, Julian Scheer

Book 6   *The Snowy Day*, Ezra Jack Keats

WHERE DOES THE SUN GO AT NIGHT?

Mirra Ginsburg

(Mulberry Books, 1981)

Where does the sun go at night? To its grandmother's house. Where does it sleep? In its grandmother's bed. Who is its grandmother? The deep, blue sky, the moon and stars and clouds. Who wakes the sun up? A red rooster!

STARTERS

Materials Needed:

1. Paper, crayons.

Procedure:

1. Check the location of the sun in the morning and again at noon, also check the time on the clock. Have children make an arc across the paper and draw in the location of the sun. Write the time (9:00 and 12:00) under each sun. Ask children to draw the sun where they think it will be in late afternoon. Ask where they think the sun goes at night?

2. Go outside and check buildings for shadows: look at your own shadow in the morning and again at noon. Make hand shadows on the wall of a building. Ask what makes a shadow. Why do we need the sun?

EXTENDERS

Materials Needed:
1. Alarm clock and automatic radio.

2. Fun Sheet from page 53, crayons, scissors.

Procedure:
1. Who wakes you up in the morning? Who wakes up your mom (dad)? Who do you think wakes the rooster up?

   Demonstrate how the alarm clock and automatic radio can be used to wake people at certain times.

2. Cut out the four cards. Draw a moon and stars on the blank card. Color the other three cards. Have children sit on the floor with their cards laid out in front of them. Instruct them to select and then hold up the card that answers these questions from the story.

   > Where does the sun go at night?
   > Where does the sun sleep at night?
   > Who is the sun's grandmother?
   > Who wakes the sun in the morning?

   Children can use the cards to retell the story. Suggest they tell the story to family members.

Book 2

GILBERTO AND THE WIND

Marie Hall Ets

(Viking, 1963)

Gilberto hears the wind and goes out to play. He watches the wind blow his balloon, the clothes drying on the line, apples off the tree, and break his umbrella. When the wind stops, he thinks it must be asleep, so he lies down and goes to sleep too.

STARTERS

Materials Needed:
   None.

Procedure:

1. We can not see the wind but we can see its action and we can hear it. Look out the window on a windy day. How can we tell the wind is blowing. Go outside and feel the force of the wind and see it's power – papers and dust blowing, trees bending. Discuss the good things about the wind – carries seeds, blows away fog and smog.

2. Recite Christina Rossetti's poem *The Wind*.

> Who has seen the wind?
> Neither you nor I.
> But when the trees bow down their heads,
> The wind is passing by.

3. Pretend you are a tree blowing in the wind; a leaf being blown by the wind; a bird trying to fly in the wind.

EXTENDERS

Materials Needed:

1. Large, envelope-style paper bags from department stores, 3-foot long pieces of string, hole punch, notebook hole reinforcers.

2. Crepe paper or newspapers, scissors.

3. Pinwheel pattern from page 56, scissors, crayons, plastic drinking straws, paper fasteners (brads).

Procedure:

1. Paper bag kite – turn down the top of the bag about 2 inches. Punch a hole through one folded side and attach a paper reinforcer over each side of the hole. Tie the string through the hole. Hold the string and run into the wind.

2. Streamer – cut 3-foot long strips of crepe paper (or colored newspapers). Hold one end of the streamer and run in the wind.

3. Give each child a pinwheel pattern. Color and then cut on the dark lines. Fold as directed. Push fastener through the center and into the top of the straw. Hold the pinwheel in front of you as you run.

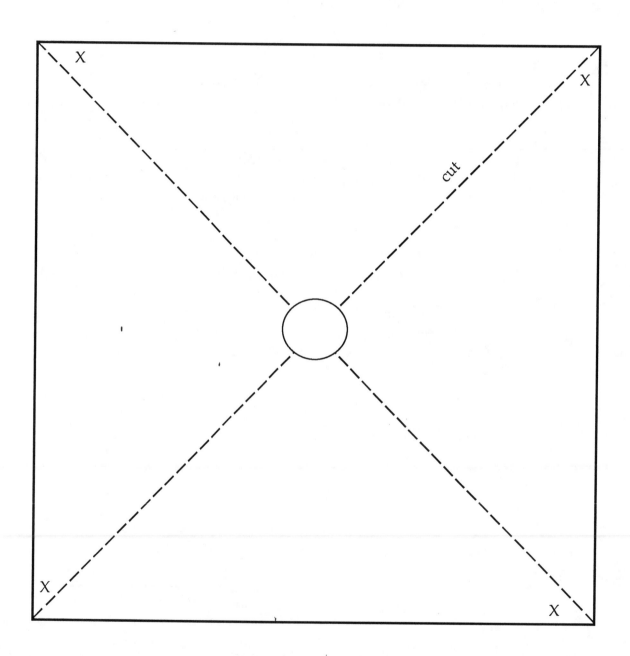

Directions:
Cut out the square. Cut on the lines. Fold corners marked "X" to center circle, overlap and insert fastener.

Book 3

IT LOOKS LIKE SPILT MILK

Charles Shaw

(Harper, 1947)

White silhouettes stand out against a bright blue background and children are invited to guess what mysterious thing it is.

The shapes resemble things they can recognize. However, it is not spilt milk, but clouds. A book to read outside under the clouds.

STARTERS

Materials Needed:
>   None.

Procedure:
>   Go outside and lie on your back on a day when white, fluffy clouds are floating about. Watch the wind blow the clouds, look for birds, airplanes and kites.

>   Does the sky look like a big blue hill? Do the clouds look like white sheep? Recite Christina Rosetti's poem *The Clouds*.

>>   White sheep, white sheep
>>   On a blue hill.
>>   When the wind stops
>>   You all stand still.

EXTENDERS

Materials Needed:
1. Long sheets of dark blue butcher paper, white, easy-to-tear paper, glue, crayons.

2. Finger paint paper, blue finger paint, glue, cotton balls, bird stickers.

Procedure:
1. Make small group murals by having children tear the white paper into large cloud shapes. Glue in place and draw in other things you might see in the sky.

2. Cover the paper with blue paint. When dry stretch the cotton balls and glue to the sky. Add bird stickers.

3. Explain that some clouds contain rain or snow. Teach the children this action rhyme:

> Rain clouds, rain clouds floating around.
> > *(Stand on tiptoe and float about)*
> Rain, rain fall to the ground.
> > *(Fall to the floor)*
> Snow clouds, snow clouds floating around.
> > *(Stand on tiptoe and float about)*
> Snow, snow fall to the ground.
> > *(Fall to the floor)*

Book 4

MUSHROOM IN THE RAIN

Mirra Ginsburg

(Macmillan, 1974)

One day ant got caught in the rain and he hid under a mushroom. Butterfly, mouse, bird, and rabbit all take refuge under the same mushroom. How is there room for all – mushrooms grow and grow where it rains.

STARTERS

Materials Needed:

Edible mushrooms, plastic serrated knife.

Procedure:

Explain that mushrooms have stems but no leaves, color or seeds. They reproduce by means of the spores. Cut mushrooms top to bottom and examine the spores.

EXTENDERS

Materials Needed:

1. Fun Sheet from page 61, tag board, scissors, stapler, crayons.

2. Large beach or patio umbrella.

Procedure:

1. Caution against eating wild mushrooms like the one in our story.

   Our mushrooms came from the market and are the kind we eat. Cut the mushrooms into bite size pieces for tasting.

2. Make several copies of the Fun Sheet on page 61 and cut apart. Children choose an animal, color it and cut out the oval. Cut 2-inch wide strips from tag board. Overlap the ends for a headband and staple to fit the child's head. Staple each child's animal to the front of their headband.

3. Children wear their headbands and stand around the room. An adult sits in the middle of the room holding the partially opened umbrella over her head. Retell the story pausing after each animal is mentioned and call that animal to come and hide under your mushroom umbrella. Continue opening the umbrella as more animals come.

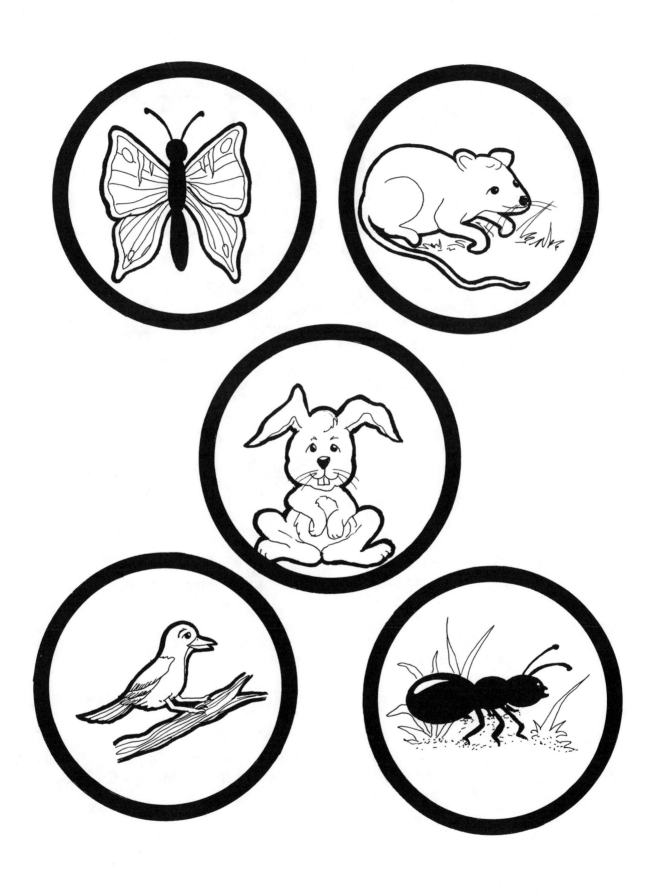

Book 5

RAIN MAKES APPLESAUCE

Julian Scheer

(Holiday House, 1964)

We need rain to make apples grow, so we can have apples for applesauce. Change of weather, seasons and changes in the apple tree. Tiny pictures in the corner of each page shows what takes place from the time the seed is planted until we have applesauce.

STARTERS

Materials Needed:

1. Large red apple with stem in a paper bag, plastic serrated knife.

2. Several red, yellow and green apples.

Procedure:

1. Hold the bag and explain that in this bag you have a little red house with no doors or windows, a chimney on top and a star inside. Ask children to guess what kind of house it is.

   Remove the house and review the description. Ask if they think there is a star inside. How can we find out?

   Cut the apple around the mid section. Both halves will contain seeds set in a star pattern.

2. Compare the apples by size and color. If we cut the apples open, what color will they be inside? Cut, examine and discuss findings. Cut bite-size pieces for a taste comparison.

EXTENDERS

Materials Needed:

1. Fun Sheet from page 64, crayons.

2. Apples from above (half apple for each child), cinnamon, nutmeg, cloves, electric skillet, sugar (optional), water, plastic serrated knives, wooden stirring spoons, potato masher, paper cups and spoons.

Procedure:

1. Fun Sheet — review the trees for each season as shown in the book.

   Directions: start with 1, (*winter*) and draw tiny branches with leaf buds; 2, (*spring*) draw tiny flowers; 3, (*summer*) a bushy tree with tiny apples; 4, (*fall*) a bushy tree with large apples and a few leaves falling to the ground.

2. Make applesauce by peeling, coring and cutting the apple into small pieces. Place in the skillet and add a small amount of water. Simmer until soft, stirring often. Cool. Mash and add sugar (if needed) and spices.

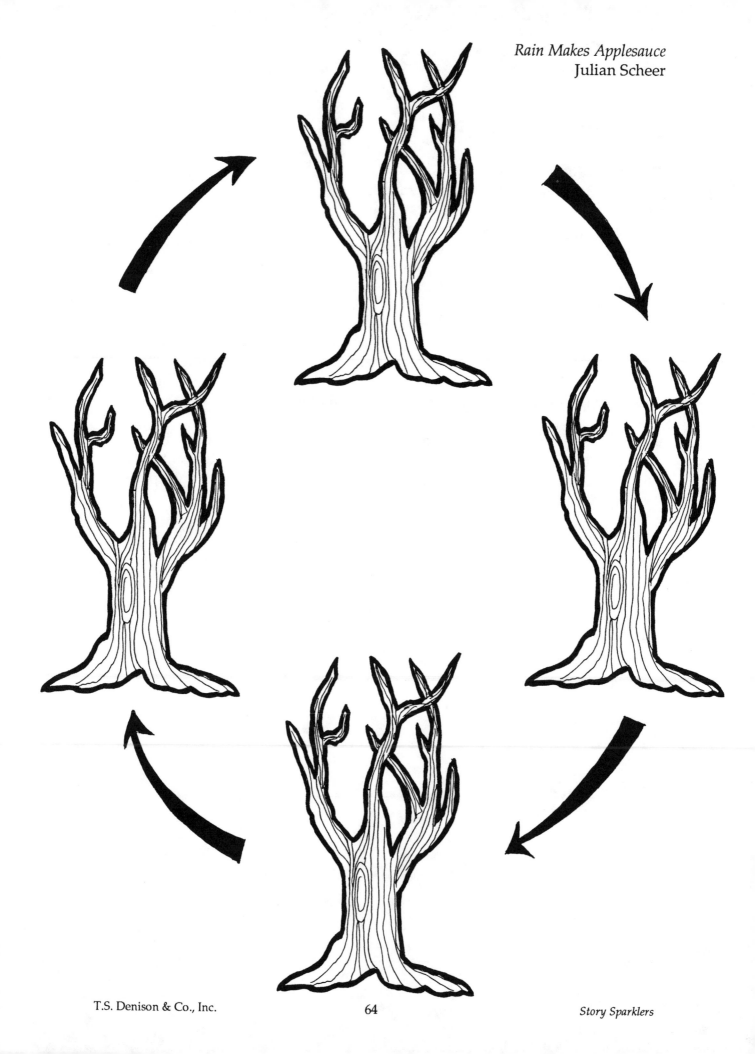

Rain Makes Applesauce
Julian Scheer

Book 6

THE SNOWY DAY

Ezra Jack Keats

(Viking, 1962)

Peter goes out in the snow alone to play. He makes foot prints, trails by dragging his feet, and angels in the snow. That night he puts a snowball in his pocket to keep for tomorrow. He awakes to a surprise!

STARTERS

Materials Needed:
1. Two snowballs (or ice cubes); 2 pockets from an old pair of blue jeans.

Procedure:
1. Place a snowball in each pocket. Put one of the pockets outside (or in a cold place). Predict which snowball will melt first.

2. Discuss how snow looks and feels, and things to do on a snowy day.

EXTENDERS

Materials Needed:
1. Scraps of cloth, paper and other collage materials, glue and sheets of paper.

Procedure:
1. Check the pockets. Discuss the results.

2. Discuss the collage illustrations in the book. Glue small scraps of material to paper to make a collage.

3. Pretend you are Peter. Let's put on our snow suit, boots, hat and mittens; open the door and go outside; make footprints in the snow; drag our feet to make two lines; pick up a stick and hit a tree; lie down and make angels in the snow; make a snowball and put it in our pocket; go inside; get undressed; take a bath; look in our pocket; go to sleep; wake up! Look out the window. What do we see?

Chapter 4
FOOD

Since most children like to eat, picture books relating to food can be used to extend your story by preparing and cooking a variety of foods. Through these food activities, children will also experience taste, smell and texture as well as color, shape and size concepts.

The Picture Books

Book 1   *Alphabet Soup*, Kate Banks

Book 2   *Bread And Jam For Frances*, Russel Hoban

Book 3   *Chicken Soup With Rice*, Maurice Sendak

Book 4   *The Duchess Bakes A Cake*, Virginia Kahl

Book 5   *If You Give A Mouse A Cookie*, Laura Numeroff

Book 6   *Peter Rabbit*, Beatrix Potter

Book 1

ALPHABET SOUP
Kate Banks
(Knopf, 1988)

A special bowl of alphabet soup takes a little boy and his bear friend on a magical adventure. Story related words magically appear as Boy dips his spoon into the bowl of soup.

STARTERS

Materials Needed:
1. Dried alphabet macaroni, clay.

2. Classroom chart and felt marker.

Procedure:
1. Set out pans of alphabet macaroni. Have children experiment with the letters, and then spell out their name. Have them shape a piece of clay and gently press in the letters.

2. Draw a soup plate on the chart and write in "ALPHABET SOUP," as shown on the book jacket.

EXTENDERS

Materials Needed:
1. Bowl, spoon and alphabet macaroni.

2. Nine, colored 3 x 5 cards, alphabet macaroni, glue

3. Fun Sheet from page 71, crayons, scissors, paper plates.

4. Cans of alphabet soup, cups, spoons, access to a stove.

Procedure:

1. Have children take turns dipping the spoon into the dry macaroni picking up one letter. Identify the letter.

2. Have children find the letters for each word – BEAR, SWORD, BOAT, NET, ROPE, TREE, CAGE, HOUSE, BED – and glue one word to each card to make a classroom set.

   Use the cards to help children learn the words. Reread the story, showing each card as the word is formed in the soup bowl. Mix up the cards and have children put them in sequence as they appeared in the story. Keep the cards on a table near the book so children can use them to retell the story.

3. Give each child a Fun Sheet to cut out. Color the bowl and finish drawing the words Boy found in his soup. Glue the bowl to the paper plate.

4. Heat and serve the alphabet soup. Let children enjoy their soup as they discover letters, tastes and smells.

Words To Be Completed

BEAR	NET	CAGE
SWORD	ROPE	HOUSE
BOAT	TREE	BED

Book 2

BREAD AND JAM FOR FRANCES

Russell Hoban

(Scholastic, 1964)

After eating only bread and jam for every meal of every day, a little badger discovers that it is fun to try other foods.

STARTERS

Materials Needed:

1. Picture of a variety of foods cut from magazines or newspaper ads, such as pancakes, cereal, spinach, ice cream.

Procedure:

1. Set out the food pictures and have each child choose one that they had for breakfast.

2. Have children share their favorite food. Then ask, "Could you eat it for each meal every day?"

EXTENDERS

Materials Needed:

1. Bread, 4 flavors of jam, paper plates, plastic knives.

2. Fun sheet from page 73, crayons, scissors.

Procedure:

1. Give each child a paper plate, knife and a slice of bread. Direct them to cut each slice of bread into 4 parts and spread each piece with a different kind of jam. Discuss smell, color and taste.

2. Give each child a Fun Sheet to cut out and fold into a sandwich. Finish drawing the letters and color the sandwich.

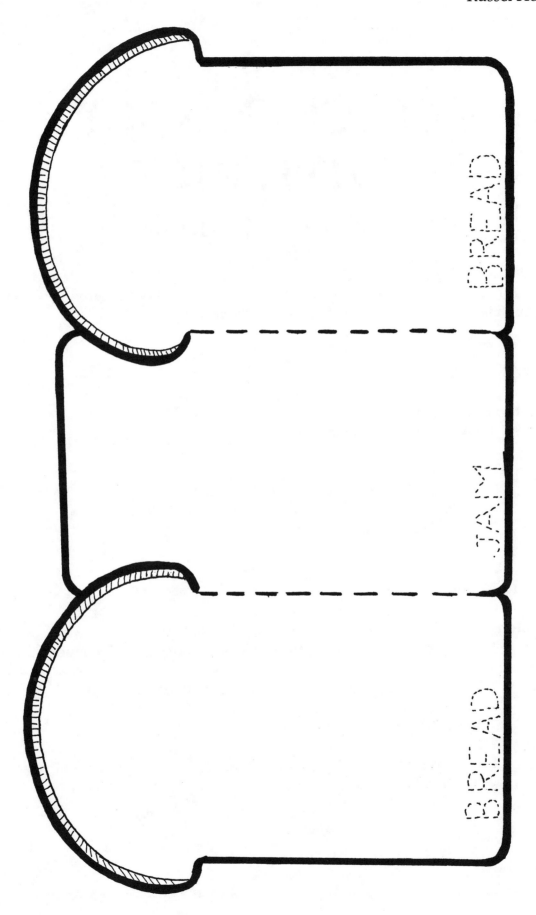

BREAD

JAM

BREAD

Book 3

CHICKEN SOUP WITH RICE
Maurice Sendak
(Harper, 1962)

A humorous book of rhymes, one for each month of the year proving that every month is a good month for chicken soup and rice.

STARTERS

Materials Needed:

1. A 12 month calendar.

Procedure:

1. Review the months of the year.

2. Recite some favorite rhymes.

EXTENDERS

Materials Needed:

1. Magazines, newspapers, toy catalogs, scissors, glue, 3 x 5 index cards.

2. Cans of chicken soup, instant rice, cups, spoons, pan, stove.

3. Fun Sheet on page 76, scissors, glue.

4. Patterns from page 77, crayons, scissors, tag board, glue, 18-inch lengths of yarn, hole punch.

Procedure:

1. Cut pictures of pairs of objects that rhyme (doll and ball) glue to the cards. Use for matching card games, have children verbalize the rhyming pairs.

2. Cook the soup and rice together according to directions on the containers. Serve the chicken soup and rice. Discuss taste, smell and texture.

3. Give each child a Fun Sheet. Chicken soup and rice go together. Cut the small strip of pictures apart and paste each one opposite the food picture it goes with.

4. Give each child a month (from the patterns) to cut out, color and paste onto tag board. Punch two holes at the top of the card and insert a piece of yarn through the holes so it can be worn around the neck.

    Duplicate the rhymes from the book to send home, or help each child learn the rhyme for their month.

    Have the children wear their neck pieces and take turns reciting their month and rhyme. The group can recite the last page together and close the presentation by pretending they are eating chicken soup and rice.

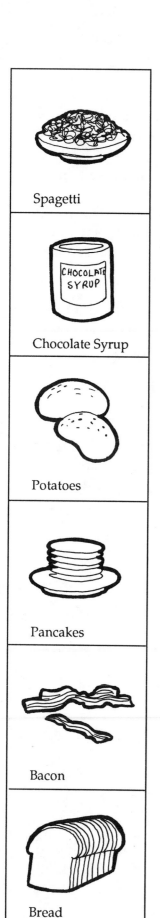

Spagetti

Chocolate Syrup

Potatoes

Pancakes

Bacon

Bread

Eggs

Butter

Gravy

Milk

Syrup

Meatballs

January

February

March

April

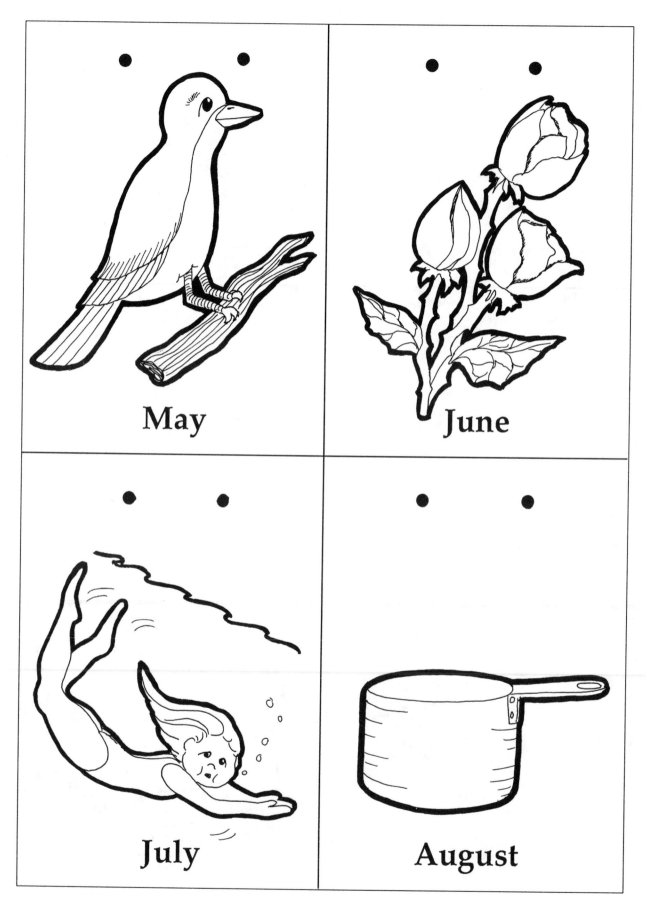

May

June

July

August

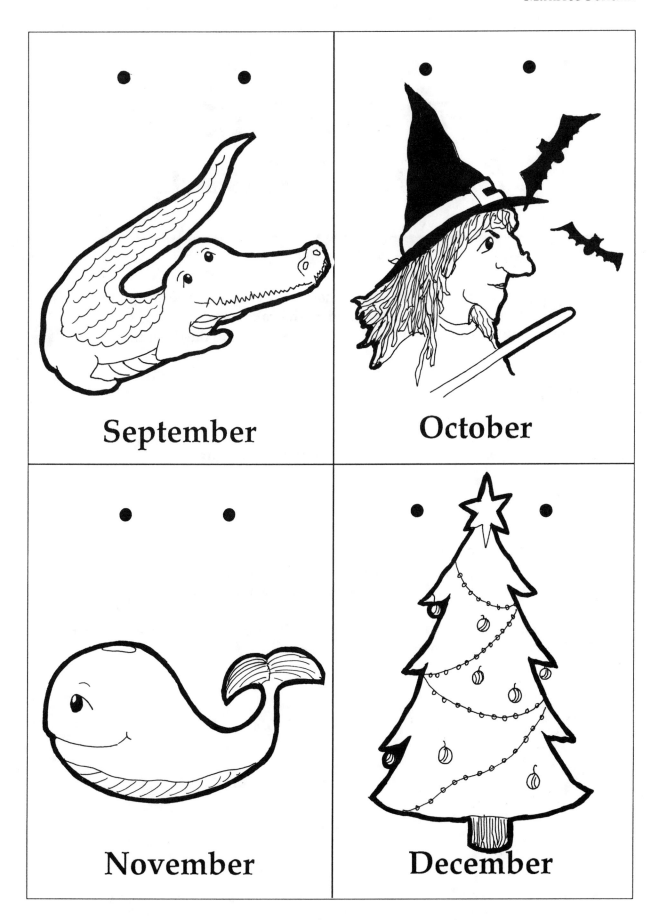

September

October

November

December

Book 4

THE DUCHESS BAKES A CAKE

Virginia Kahl

(Scribner, 1955)

A rhyming nonsense story about a duchess who decides to bake a cake. She adds the yeast six times for good measure and as the cake rises, she rises with it. Her youngest daughter comes up with a "delicious" solution to the dilemma.

STARTERS

Materials Needed:

1. Cake pans in assorted shapes (aluminum foil pans).

2. Box of cake mix.

Procedure:

1. Identify the shape of each pan. Find objects in the room that are the same shape as each pan. Take a vote on which pan children would use if they were to bake a cake. Decide which cake shape is the most popular.

2. Read the direction from a box of cake mix. Ask why they think the company put the directions on the box.

EXTENDERS

Materials Needed:

1. Two boxes of cake mix (utensils and ingredients listed on the box), sheet pan, miniature cup cake tins, plastic knives, paper plates, powdered sugar, milk, food coloring, bowls, plastic spoons, measuring teaspoons and tablespoons.

2. Two or three packages of rapid rising yeast, measuring cup, spoon.

3. Tape, felt marker, for each child, a 4 x 12 card cut from tag board.

Procedure:

1. Prepare and bake the cake and cupcakes according to directions (save a small bowl of cake batter). Cut the cake when cool. Each child needs a cup cake, a piece of sheet cake, knife, bowl and spoon.

   Measure and mix 3 tablespoons of powdered sugar into a bowl. Slowly stir in one teaspoon (or more) of milk until mixture is spreadable. Tint with food coloring and spread on the cake and cup cake. Before eating, cut the cake into other geometric shapes. Take turns identifying the shapes on each plate.

2. Remind the children that our cake did not contain any yeast like the Duchess's cake. Let's see what would happen if we added yeast to the cake batter we saved. Mix the yeast according to directions, stir into the batter and find out!

3. Write, "Our cakes tastes" on a card and tape it to the wall. Have each child add one word to describe our cake. Write it on a card and tape it following the first card. Reread the sentence as each new word is added.

Book 5

IF YOU GIVE A MOUSE A COOKIE

Laura Numeroff

(Harper, 1985)

What will happen if you give a mouse a cookie? We are told the mouse would probably ask for a glass of milk, a straw, a napkin, a mirror and several other items. Near the end of the story, mouse would want to take a nap, which would lead to a story and eventually to another cookie.

STARTERS

Materials Needed:

1. A glass of milk and a cookie.

2. Cookies in different geometric shapes.

Procedure:

1. Set out the milk and cookies. Ask who they think this snack is for.

2. Ask children to share their favorite kind of cookie. Show and identify the shapes of the cookies. Let them tell which shape they would give a mouse and why.

EXTENDERS

Materials Needed:

1. Chocolate chip, oatmeal and raisin cookies and vanilla wafers, milk, cups.

2. Use of an oven, cookie sheet, knife and package of slice and bake refrigerator cookies.

3. Mouse puppet pattern from page 84, scissors, crayons, glue.

4. Jar of paint and paint brush, pencil and piece of paper, cup and saucer, plastic needle and spool of thread, empty soda can and plastic straw, book and bookmark.

Procedure:

1. Identify the cookie flavors. Break cookies in half for a taste test, and serve the milk. Compare the taste, smell and texture.

2. Slice and bake the cookies according to the directions on the package. Eat! Compare to the cookies above.

3. Copy the mouse puppet onto heavy construction paper. Give each child two to color and cut out. Glue the edges of the two mice together, leaving the bottom open to slip over your finger.

4. Set out the go-together items at random. Have each child wear their mouse puppet, answer with the missing word and then place the two items together. Ask, "If you give your mouse a jar of paint, it will ask for a . . ." (paint brush).

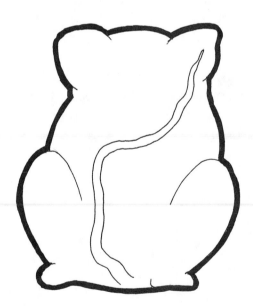

Directions:
Cut two, glue edges together, leaving the bottom open to slip over your fingers.

Book 6

PETER RABBIT

Beatrix Potter

(Warne, undated)

Peter has a daring adventure in Mr. McGregor's garden, but returns safely home where his mother gives him a cup of camomile tea and tucks him into bed.

STARTERS

Materials Needed:

1. Carrots, turnips, beets, radishes, plastic knife.

2. Fresh, plastic, or pictures of vegetables.

Procedure:

1. Cut the tops along with a half-inch of the vegetable from carrots, turnips, beets, radishes. Keep the root part hidden. Show the tops and have children try to identify each vegetable. Set out the vegetables and have them match tops to roots.

2. Before children arrive, place the vegetables about the room. Describe the vegetables, one at a time, and have the group name the vegetables.

   Give directions for finding one of the vegetables to one child at a time, such as "Go to the window, turn right and look up."

EXTENDERS

Materials Needed:

1. Vegetable tops from above, colored ink pads, paper.

2. Fun Sheet from page 87, scissors, glue, large sheet of paper, wax paper, stapler.

3. Camomile tea, tea pot, cups, vegetables from above, lettuce, cabbage or other vegetables, napkins.

Procedure:

1. Use the vegetable tops as stamps to make designs.

2. Give each child a Fun Sheet. Color the vegetables and tops, cut them out and glue to the large sheet of paper matching tops to the vegetables. Cover the paper with a sheet of wax paper. Staple the edges together and trim excess wax paper. Use as a placemat.

3. Have a tea party. Make camomile tea. Clean and cut the vegetables into bite size pieces. Use the placemats.

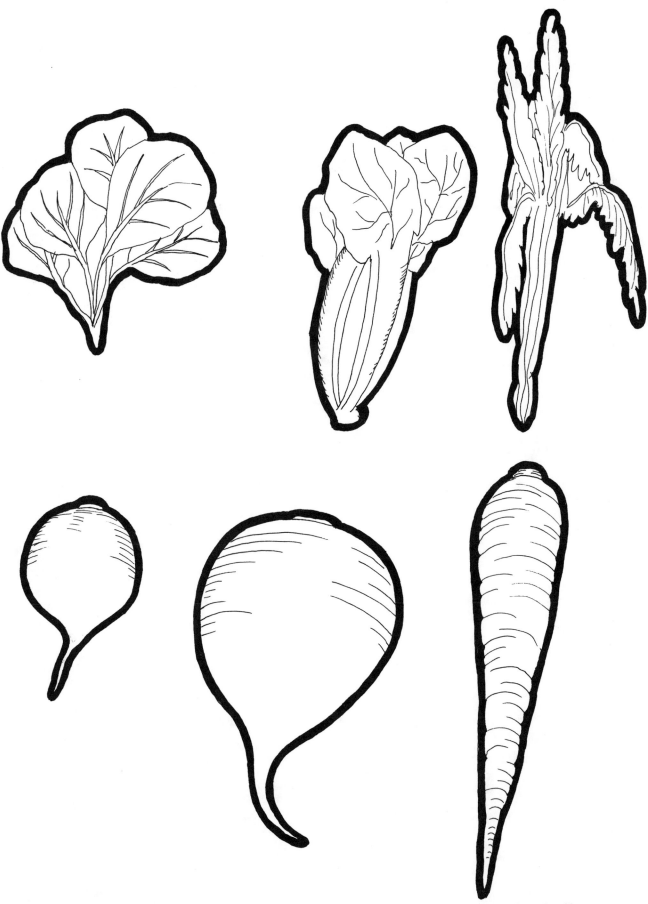

Chapter 5
ANIMALS

Most children seem to relate well to animals. Using picture books where the main character is an animal will help children understand many human problems and needs, and will give them an understanding of specific animals, their needs and care and why they are important to the balance of nature.

The Picture Books

Book 1   *Crictor*, Tomi Ungerer

Book 2   *Dinosaur Time*, Peggy Parish

Book 3   *Frederick*, Leo Lionni

Book 4   *I'm In The Zoo, Too*, Brent Ashabranner

Book 5   *Little Chicken*, Margaret Wise Brown

Book 6   *Mo Mo's Kitten*, Mitsu and Tara Yashima

CRICTOR

Tomi Ungerer

(Harper, 1958)

Mrs. Bodot, the local school teacher, receives a present in the mail from her son (a snake). She takes Crictor the snake to school and he helps the children learn by forming his body into letters, numerals, tying knots and playing with them. And what does clever Crictor do when a burglar enters the house?

STARTERS

Materials Needed:

1. Different lengths of yarn in a variety of colors.

2. A box, containing a toy snake (or picture of a snake), wrapped in brown paper, addressed to Mrs. Bodot.

Procedure:

1. Set out the pieces of yarn and challenge children to form letters, numerals and geometric shapes.

2. Let children handle and examine the box, and then guess what is inside. Slowly open the box as you start to read the book, revealing the snake at the appropriate time.

EXTENDERS

Materials Needed:

1. Playdough in different colors; yarn, plastic drinking straws, scissors.

Procedure:

1. Use the playdough to form snakes. Cut the straws in pieces and string on a piece of yarn. Knot the ends to make a snake.

2. Have children stand and form their bodies into various shapes, and letters (X, C, D, Y, F, I, J, L work well). Lie on the floor and repeat the process.

Book 2

DINOSAUR TIME
Peggy Parish
(Harper Trophy, 1974)

Excellent pictures, descriptions and information on eleven dinosaurs including a pronunciation guide. No one has ever seen a dinosaur but scientists are finding out how they lived, what they ate and what they looked like.

STARTERS

Materials Needed:
1. None

2. Class chart and marking pen.

Procedure:
1. Sing Ten Little Dinosaurs to the tune of Ten Little Indians.

2. Ask children for the names of some dinosaurs. Write the names on the class chart.

EXTENDERS

Materials Needed:

1. Large piece of heavy cardboard cut from an appliance box, green, brown and blue paint, paint brushes. Dinosaur patterns from page 95, scissors, crayons or paint, glue.

2. None.

Procedure:

1. Paint the cardboard making a water, grass and dirt area. Make copies of the dinosaur patterns on heavy paper and cut them out. Color or paint both sides of each dinosaur. When dry, bend and glue the tabs to the cardboard so the animals will stand for a classroom dino-zoo.

2. Creative movement – Pretend you are a very big dinosaur plodding through the water; a tiny dinosaur with a long neck eating leaves from a tree; a short, fat dinosaur walking through the tall grass. Let children offer suggestions.

Book 3

FREDERICK

Leo Lionni

(Knopf/Pantheon, 1967)

A family of five field mice lived in a rock wall. They gathered food for the winter, all but Frederick who seems to always be dreaming. But his surprise brings warmth and joy when all the food is gone and the house is cold. The story ends with a poem. Contains simple torn-page illustrations.

STARTERS

Materials Needed:
1. None.

2. None.

Procedure:
1. Ask children for a definition of "imagination."
   While children close their eyes, recite "Hickery Dickery Dock" in a slow whisper. Ask them to share the pictures they saw in their minds.

2. Close your eyes. See the bright sun shinning. See the beautiful colors of a rainbow. See a book filled with words. (These are things Frederick sees).

EXTENDERS

Materials Needed:

1. Construction paper in shades of brown, blue, gray, and white, glue.

2. Mouse pattern from page 98, gray and brown felt, scissors, glue, gray or brown yarn, stapler, felt-tipped marker.

Procedure:

1. Discuss the illustrations in the book. Explain that they are made using torn paper. Children can tear paper rocks and mice, arrange them on a sheet of white paper and glue in place.

2. Use the pattern to cut 2 mice from felt. Glue the two mice together, leaving the bottom open. Staple on a yarn tail and glue the ears in place Draw in the nose and eyes.

   Wear the mouse puppet and recite "Hickery Dickery Dock."

   Take turns pretending you are Frederick and say, "Close your eyes and see the . . ."

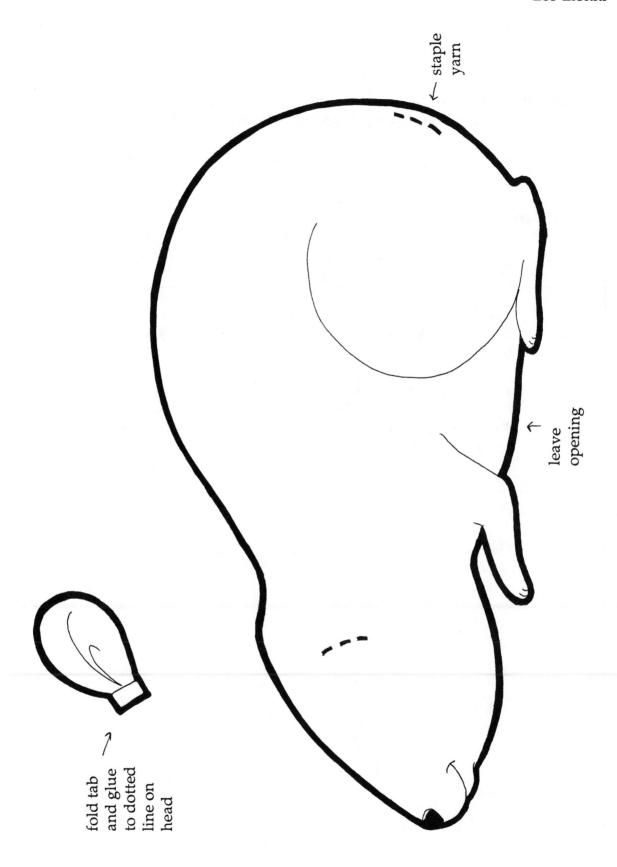

Frederick
Leo Lionni

staple
yarn

leave
opening

fold tab
and glue
to dotted
line on
head

Book 4

I'M IN THE ZOO, TOO
Brent Ashabranner
(Cobblehill/Dutton, 1989)

A little squirrel and his family live in the zoo, but he wants to be in the zoo and get fed, do tricks and have people take pictures of him. After getting locked in a cage overnight, the little squirrel decides he likes living in the zoo, but no longer wants to be in the zoo like the other animals.

STARTERS

Materials Needed:
1. Assorted plastic animals (or pictures) including, zoo, farm and pet animals.

2. Shoe boxes, yarn, stuffed or other toy animals.

Procedure:
1. Discuss the zoo, animals that live in the zoo and childrens' favorite zoo animals. Sort the animals into groups – zoo, farm, pets.

2. Set up a zoo by collecting animals from the classroom (or use picture) that might live in a zoo. Stand the shoe boxes on end, place the animals inside and wrap yarn around the box to form cages.

EXTENDERS

Material Needed:
1. Stuffed or plastic zoo animals.

2. Squirrel pattern from page 101, small paper lunch bags, scissors, crayons, glue.

Procedure:
1. Choose one of the animals and show me what kind of tricks you would do if you were in the zoo.

2. Copy the squirrel pattern onto paper. Color and cut out. To make a paper bag puppet, glue the top of the squirrel's head to the bottom section of the paper bag. Glue the bottom half underneath so the mouth can be open and closed. Use the puppets to retell the story.

Paper bag puppet to be glued to a lunch bag lying flat. The top of the head is glued to the bottom section of the bag; the bottom of the head is glued underneath the bottom section of the bag so the mouth can be opened and closed.

Book 5

LITTLE CHICKEN
Margaret Wise Brown
(Harper, 1943)

Little chicken belongs to a rabbit. One day the rabbit wanted to run and run. So the little chicken went to find someone else to play with. He found some who did and some who did not want to play. When the sun went down, rabbit ran home to chicken and chicken ran home to rabbit.

STARTERS

Materials Needed:
1. Shoe box, ribbon, stuffed, toy rabbit and chicken. Place the animals in the box and tie with the ribbon.

2. Rabbit and chicken from above.

Procedure:
1. Handle and shake the box and try to guess its contents. Remove the ribbon and open the box.

2. Use the animals as you teach the rhymes below. Have children use their fingers to show the correct number as they join in.

   RABBIT
   Five little rabbits sitting in the sun.
   Four little rabbits having lots of fun.
   Three little rabbits, what have they done?
   Two little rabbits played tag and won.
   One little rabbit takes off on a run. Run, run, run!

CHICKEN

One little chicken watching a hawk.
Four little chickens playing with chalk.
Three little chickens trying to talk.
Two little chickens stretching to gawk.
One little chicken taking a walk. Walk, walk, walk!

EXTENDERS

Materials Needed:

1. Rabbit and chicken patterns from page 104, white cardboard, crayons, toilet tissue spools cut in half, scissors, glue cotton batting and yellow art feathers.

2. Fun Sheet maze from page 105, pencil.

Procedure:

1. Trace the patterns onto cardboard. Cut out, color and glue one piece of each animal to opposite ends of two spools to make a stand-up rabbit and chicken. Glue cotton to the rabbit and feathers to the chicken.

   Use the animals as you repeat the rhymes above.

2. A Fun Sheet from page 105 for each child. Help chicken find his way through the maze and back to rabbit.

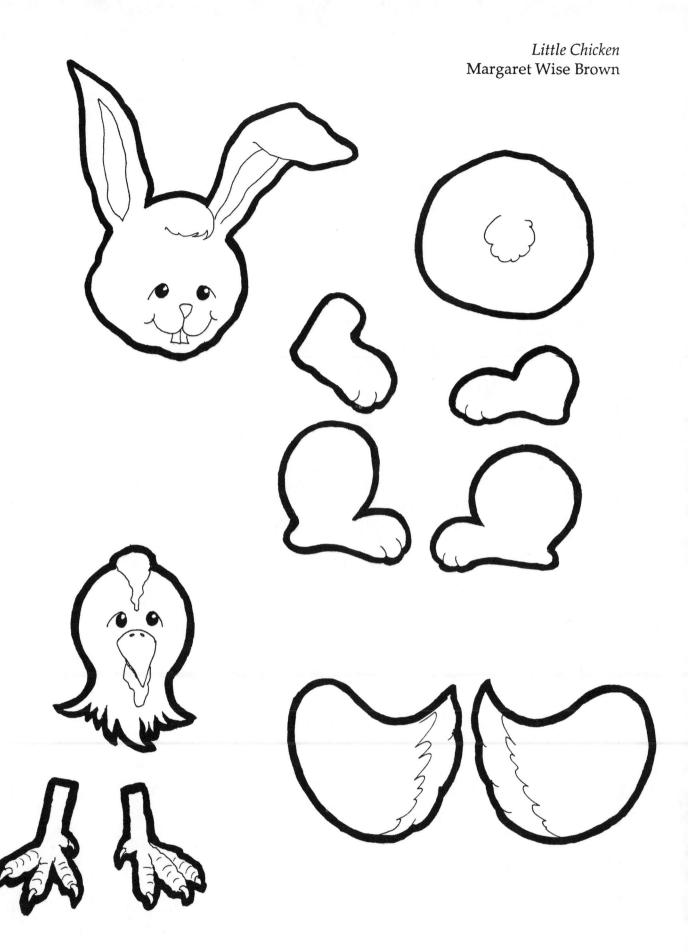

A pencil maze of paths that will take chicken back to rabbit.

Book 6

MOMO'S KITTEN
Mitsu and Taro Yashima
(Viking, 1961)

Momo finds a kitten. The kitten grows up and has five kittens. They eat, play and grow. Momo can not keep them. She must give them away. Momo is sad, but then she discovers her beautiful mother cat will soon have kittens again.

STARTERS

Materials Needed:

1. Have someone bring in a friendly cat in a pet carrier for children to observe for a short time.

2. Hand mirrors.

Procedure:

1. Observe the cat move, play, eat, drink, have the cat's owner tell about the needs and care of the cat.

2. Look closely at the shape and color of the cat's eyes. Look in the mirror at your eyes. Discuss the differences and similarities.

EXTENDERS

Materials Needed:
1. None.

2. Kitten pattern from page 108, light weight paper, scissors, crayons.

3. Paper bag, fake fur, several broom straws tied together (whiskers), bone (claws), heavy craft cording (tail).

Procedure:
1. Have a pet day where children bring in what they think would be the best pet in the world (stuffed or toy animals or a picture). Count the pets, classify them, and discuss why they think their animals would be the best pet.

2. Accordion pleat the paper, trace the kitten pattern, and then cut out. Color one side of each kitten and write your name for the kitten on the other side.

3. Place the items in the bag. Feel and find something that feels like kitten's body; kitten's whiskers; kitten's claws; kitten's tail.

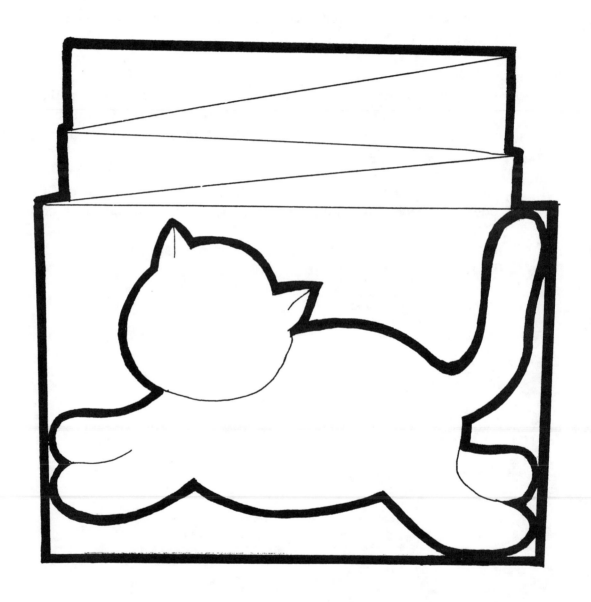

Chapter 6
TRANSPORTATION

Books relating to transportation can help young children learn about various vehicles, what they do and how they provide for our travel needs.

The Picture Books

Book 1   *Boats*, Byron Barton

Book 2   *How Many Are In This Old Car*, Colin & Jacqui Hawkins

Book 3   *If I Drove A Train*, Miriam Young

Book 4   *If I Flew A Plane*, Miriam Young

Book 5   *School Bus*, Donald Crews

Book 6   *Trucks*, Donald Crews

BOATS

Byron Barton

(Crowell, 1986)

Good pictures of boats – rowboat, sailboat, ferryboat, fishing boat, tugboat, motorboat, fireboat and a cruise ship. Each page has one sentence telling the job of each boat.

STARTERS

Materials Needed:
1. None.

2. Pieces of colored yarn each about 6' long.

Procedure:
1. "I'm thinking of something that moves about on the water. Sometimes it goes fast; sometimes slow." If children can not guess your riddle, give additional clues describing boats. Share and discuss boating experiences.

2. Use the yarn to form boat outlines on the floor. Sit in your boat and row it as you sing "Row Row, Row Your Boat."

EXTENDERS

Materials Needed:
1. Wading pool filled with water, styrofoam egg cartons (cut the cups apart), toothpicks, tape, clay, scissors, white paper, crayons.

2. Material from above, yellow, white, blue, and pink egg cartons, large piece of blue butcher paper cut into an oval.

3. Fun Sheet from page 113, crayons.

Procedure:

1. Cut a small sail from the paper and color it. Tape it to a toothpick. Press a small amount of clay into the bottom of the egg cup. Push the toothpick into the clay only. Float your boat.

   Have a race by blowing the boats across the water.

2. Make several boats in your choice of colors. Set them out on the paper lake. Sort the colors into groups. Math examples: Which color group has the most boats? Are there more pink or yellow boats? How many yellow boats do we need to add to make the groups equal? If 3 yellow boats sail away, how many yellow boats will be left?

3. Give each child a Fun Sheet and crayons. Draw a line from the word to the matching boat. On the back of the page, draw your favorite boat.

sailboat

tugboat

ferryboat

fishing boat

motorboat

fireboat

rowboat

cruise ship

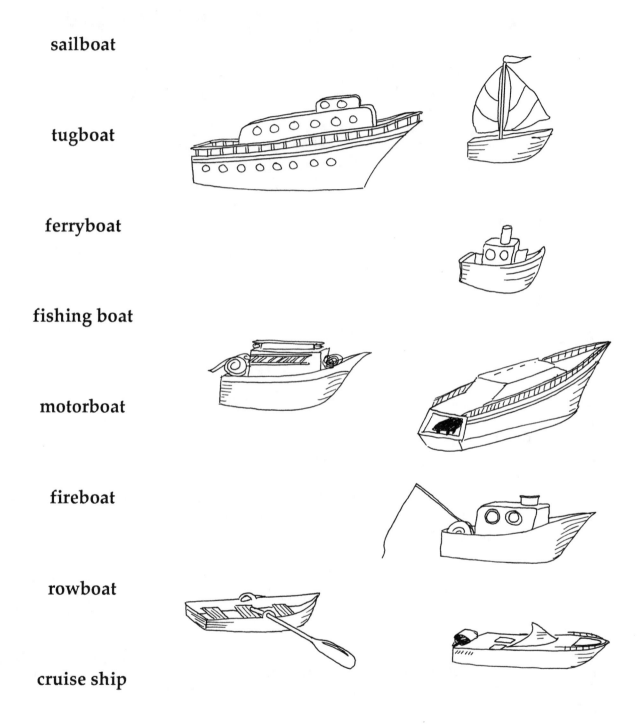

Book 2

HOW MANY ARE IN THIS OLD CAR?

Colin and Jacqui Hawkins
(Putnam, 1988)

A rhyming, counting book about bear going for a ride in his very old, open-air car. One at a time, nine of his friends want to join him, but he fears the car will break if they do. And that is just what happens?

STARTERS

Materials Needed:

1. None

2. Rope (6' to 8' long), a sheet of red and green paper.

Procedure:

1. Have children use their fingers as they count 1 to 10; and 10 to 1.

   As you call out the words, have children show you the number of fingers that rhymes with the word – fun (one), you, more, me, heaven, then, drive, fine, weight, mix.

2. Let children use the rope to form an outline of a car on the floor. Tie ends of rope together. Count out ten children to get into the car. Is there room? Squeeze in!

   Hold onto the rope with one hand. When you see the green card, stand and walk around the room; when you see a red card, stop and sit down.

EXTENDERS

Materials Needed:
1. Finger puppet patterns from page 116 & 117, scissors, tape, crayons.

2. Fun Sheet from page 118, crayons.

3. Check with local automobile dealers for car pictures and collect magazines that contain cars, large sheet of paper, pencils or crayons, glue.

Procedure:
1. Color and cut out the finger puppets. Cut the tabs to overlap and fit your finger. Tape in place.

   Place one puppet on each finger as you count 1 to 10; remove one puppet at a time as you count 10 to 1.

   Call out the rhyming words above and have them place the **rhyming** number of puppets on their fingers.

2. Color the **number** of animals faces that rhymes with the word below the picture. Write the correct numeral in the blank after the word.

3. Look through car brochures and magazines to find a picture of a car that looks like your family car.

   Identify different kinds of cars and spell out the names (station wagon, sedan and so on).

   Cut out pictures of three of your favorites, paste to a sheet of paper. Copy the name of the car under the picture.

117

Book 3

IF I DROVE A TRAIN
Miriam Young
(Lothrop, 1972)

Discover about trains as a boy shows why he wants to drive a train when he grows up. Pictures show different kinds of trains and tunnels, subways and bridges as the trains travel along their routes.

STARTERS

Materials Needed:
1. None.

2. Invite a train buff to visit and bring his train and uniform or invite a friend who has a train set.

    A cut-out paper train engine, crayons.

Procedure:
1. What would you like to be when you grow up?

    What would you do if your job was to drive a train?

2. Have all the children write their names on the train engine picture.

    Welcome your guest speaker.

    Present the thank-you train engine picture to your guest and sing "A big thank-you to you. . ." to the tune of Happy Birthday.

EXTENDERS

Materials Needed:

1. Check with the local Amtrack station or a travel agent for pictures of trains, large sheet of butcher paper, paint and brushes.

2. Collect small boxes, paint and brushes, safe object for punching holes, yarn (optional: cardboard circles for wheels and paper brads).

3. Classroom chairs, tag board, stapler, paper, hole punch, visor hat pattern from page 121.

4. Fun Sheet from page 122, pencils or crayons.

Procedure:

1. Paint a large train track the length of the paper. Add a bridge, trestle and tunnel. Cut out the trains and glue them along the track. Identify the cars.

2. Paint the boxes. For a train, punch holes in both ends of the boxes. Place the boxes end to end and string them on the yarn. Knot both ends. (Optional: attach 4 wheels to each box with paper brads).

3. Set up the chairs to form the passenger car. Take turns as the conductor and engineer.

   Overlap the ends of the headband to fit your head and staple together. Bend the cap bill on the dotted line and staple the straight end to the center of the headband.

   Make paper tickets to pass out and punch as passengers board the train.

4. Dot-to-dot Fun Sheet for each child to complete.

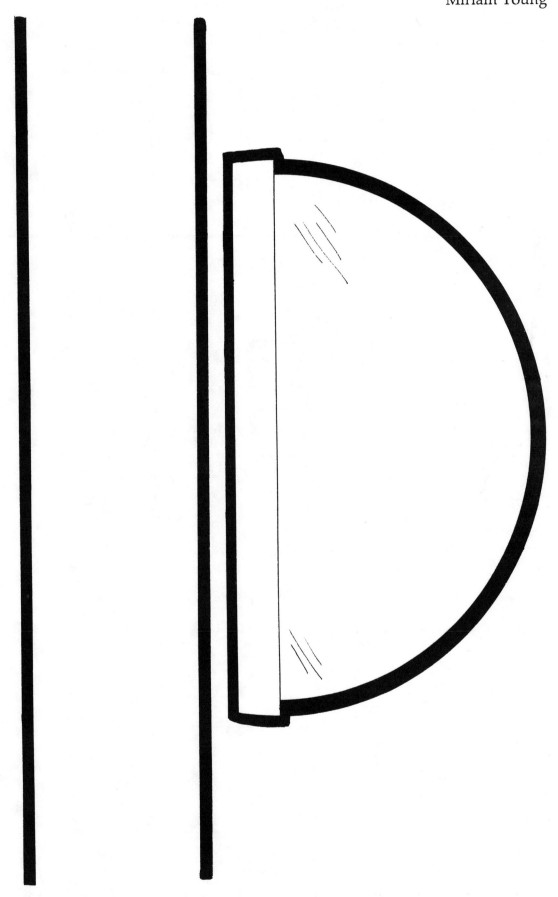

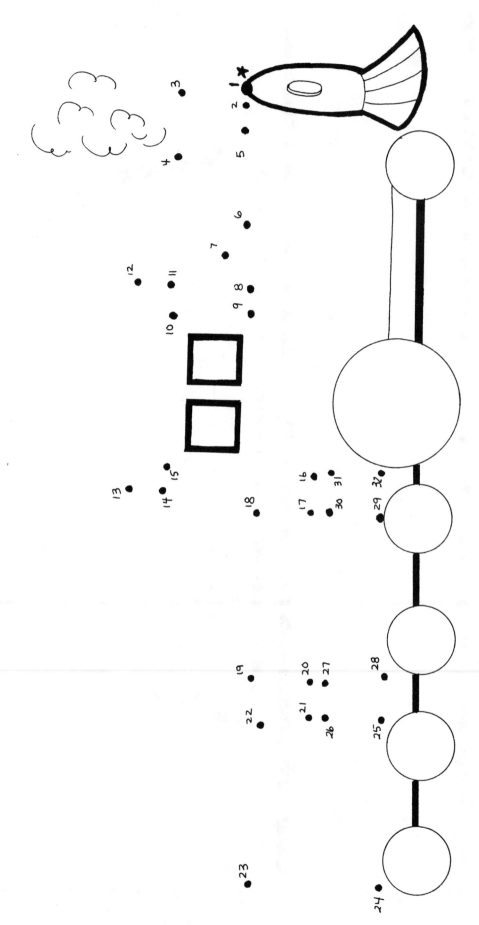

Book 4

IF I FLEW A PLANE

Miriam Young

(Lothrop, 1970)

A young boy decides he will fly a plane when he grows up, but what kind will he fly? He takes us on a trip in different kinds of flying machines – passenger, cargo, stunt, private, seaplane, glider, helicopter, and a space ship. After telling about all the things he will do while flying, he decides maybe he will take turns flying each one of them . . . and he may even invent one of his own.

STARTERS

Materials Needed:
1. World globe.

2. None.

Procedure:
1. Where would you go if you could fly a plane? Locate each place on the globe.

2. Discuss trips children have made by plane; what they did to get ready; where they went; what they saw; and what they think an airline pilot does.

EXTENDERS

Materials Needed:
1. Pattern from page 125, sheets of white paper, crayons.

2. Half sheets of white paper, classroom building blocks, lengths of yarn.

3. Strips of corrugated cardboard, glue, safe object for punching hole, string, scissors.

Procedure:
1. Choose an airplane pattern. Draw designs on your paper. Follow the folding directions. Fly the planes.

2. Dramatic play – fold and make three airplanes using the half sheets of paper. Use the blocks and pieces of yarn to build an airport, hangers and runways.

3. Cut one strip of cardboard to make the plane's body and another for the wings. Glue the wings in place. Punch a hole in the center front section and attach a piece of string. Go outside, hold the end of the string, and fly your plane.

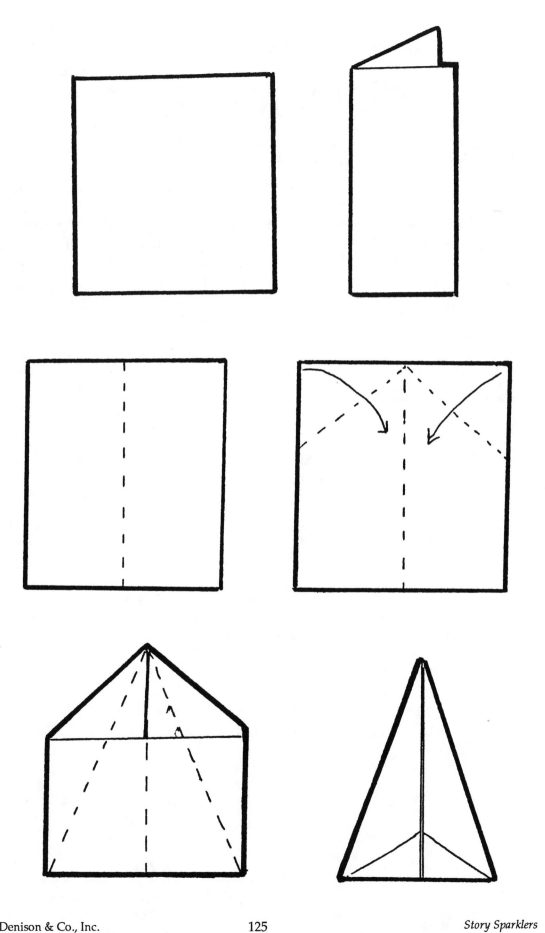

Book 5

SCHOOL BUS
Donald Crews
(Greenwillow, 1984)

Large and small, yellow school buses start off from their parking area empty. They cross town, pick up children and take them to school. Then the empty buses wait, pick up the children, take them home and again return empty to the parking area. The large pictures and short text give a good introduction to the school bus and what it does.

STARTERS

Materials Needed:
1. None.

2. Poster board, felt marker, small squares of paper in yellow (bus), blue (car), red (walk), green (other), glue.

Procedure:
1. Riddle – What is large (or small), bright yellow, and filled with students? (Found inside book jacket.)

   Sing "The Wheels On the Bus Go 'Round and 'Round."

2. Ask how many ride the school bus; come by car; walk; other means.

   Discuss city buses, streetcars and other types of buses.

   Make a classroom graph – bus, car, walk, other. Have each student choose the appropriate color of paper for how they get to school and glue in place on the graph.

EXTENDERS

Materials Needed:

1. Large rectangle appliance box for bus body, smaller box for motor area, sharp knife for adult use, heavy duty duct tape, paint and brushes, classroom chairs.

2. Fun Sheet from page 128, pencils or crayons.

Procedure:

1. Lay the big box on its side. Cut and remove top and the window and windshield area. Cut two sides of the door and bend open. Tape the smaller box to the front of the bus. Paint the bus. Paint in wheels, front grill, lights and other details.

   Set chairs inside. Take turns being the driver. Discuss good manners for bus riders.

2. Give each child a Fun Sheet maze and pencil or crayon. Help the bus find its way from the parking area to the school.

Book 6

TRUCKS

Donald Crews

(Greenwillow, 1980)

A wordless book that uses signs and pictures to illustrate different kinds of trucks and their travels. One truck carries a special surprise load!

STARTERS

Materials Needed:

1. Pictures (cut from magazines or from a truck dealer's brochure) of different kinds of trucks – freight, mail, U.P.S., moving van, pickup, stock, delivery, water, fire.

2. Toy trucks, pictures from above.

Procedure:

1. Lay the pictures upside down on the table. Children can choose one, identify by the type, and then tell what the truck might carry.

2. Set out the toy trucks and pictures. Match trucks to pictures.

EXTENDERS

Materials Needed:

1. Butcher paper, finger paint, truck pictures from above.

2. Patterns of road signs from page 131, 3 x 5 cards, scissors, glue.

3. Classroom unit blocks, toy cars, road signs, lengths of yarn, drinking straws.

Procedure:

1. Cover the butcher paper with fingerpaint. With hands and fingers, draw roads, bridges, overpasses, tunnels, gas station, railroad crossing and stop lights. When dry, glue pictures of trucks on the roads.

2. Cut out and glue the road signs to the bottom half of the cards. Help children learn to recognize and identify the road signs.

3. Make roads using unit blocks, yarn and straws. Fold the road sign cards in half so they will stand and set them up along the roads. Drive toy cars and trucks obeying the signs.

Chapter 7

FAMILIES

These books about families and family members will give young children a better understanding of their relationship to the people who make up their immediate family as well as their extended family.

The Picture Books

Book 1   *Blueberries For Sal*, Robert McCloskey

Book 2   *Jennie's Hat*, Ezra Jack Keats

Book 3   *Nana Upstairs & Nana Downstairs*, Tomi de Paola

Book 4   *On Mother's Lap*, Ann Herbert Scott

Book 5   *Peter's Chair*, Ezra Jack Keats

Book 6   *Staying With Grandma*, Eileen Roe

BLUEBERRIES FOR SAL

Robert McCloskey

(Viking, 1984)

A little girl and a baby bear are out hunting blueberries with their mothers. Sal likes the sound of each berry as she drops it into her pail. While busy eating berries, Sal and the little bear suddenly discover they have been following the wrong mother. However, they are soon reunited with their own mother. Illustrations are in blue and white.

STARTERS

Materials Needed:
1. Fresh, frozen and canned blueberries, small paper plates.

2. Three containers (cardboard, plastic, metal), 3 large paper bags, marble, wood bead, small plastic bead to represent a blueberry.

Procedure:
1. Serve three blueberries, one of each type. Observe. Discuss shape, texture, smell, taste, and compare differences.

2. Examine the containers and other items. Children take turns choosing one of the objects (keep it hidden) and dropping it into the metal container. Other children try to identify the object by sound.

   Place a container inside each bag. Children take turns dropping the small plastic bead (blueberry) into one of the cans. Other children try to identify the container by sound.

EXTENDERS

Materials Needed:

1. Blueberry juice, large coffee filter papers, medicine droppers, small bowls.

2. Package of blueberry muffin mix, and utensils required according to directions on the box, small muffin tins, stove, napkins.

3. Classroom chart and felt markers.

Procedure:

1. Pour small amount of juice into the bowls. Fold the coffee filters several times. Drop juice on the folded filter to make designs. Carefully unfold and let dry.

2. Mix, bake and serve the muffins. Discuss the taste.

3. Make a list on the chart of other ways we could use blueberries – pies, jam, on cereal.

Book 2

JENNIE'S HAT
Ezra Jack Keats
(Harper, 1966)

Jennie's aunt sends her a new hat as a present. She is disappointed with the new hat because it is only a plain hat. She wants a beautiful, fancy, flowery hat. It is the birds, that Jennie feeds every Saturday, that help change her plain hat into a beautifully decorated one.

STARTERS

Materials Needed:
1. Classroom chart, felt marker.

2. A plain straw hat.

Procedure:
1. Explain the relationship of an aunt. Make and ABC chart to show A for aunt; B for brother; C for cousin; D for dad; G for grandma and grandpa; M for mother; S for sister; U for uncle. Help children learn to recognize the words.

2. Wear the hat. Is this the most beautiful, fanciest, loveliest hat you have ever seen?

    What could we do to this hat to make it fancy and beautiful?

EXTENDERS

Materials Needed:
1. Collection boxes (for hat decorations).

2. Large paper plates, hole punch, yarn, scissors, staplers, glue.

3. Marching music.

Procedure:
1. Have children help collect recyclable items – ribbons, old holiday decorations, feathers, dried and plastic leaves and flowers and gift wrapping paper. Discuss recycling.

2. Punch two holes on opposite sides of a paper plate. Attach two pieces of yarn long enough to knot and then tie under your chin. Decorate your hat with material from the collection box.

   Ask each child for a word that describes their hat.

3. Play marching music and have a hat parade.

Book 3

NANA UPSTAIRS & NANA DOWNSTAIRS

Tomi de Paola

(Putnam, 1973)

Tommy has a grandmother who lives downstairs and a great grandmother who lives upstairs in the same house. Tommy loves them both and visits them every Sunday. He runs upstairs and downstairs entertaining and being entertained.

STARTERS

Materials Needed:
1. Yellow and blue 3 x 5 cards, felt marker.

2. Cards made in #1 below.

Procedure:
1. Ask each child for the name they call their grandmother (or another relative) and write it on two matching cards. Give the blue card to the child and keep the yellow one.

2. Lay out the yellow "grandma" cards face up on the floor, and let each child find the yellow card that matches theirs.

    Collect the yellow cards and read off the names. As the children recognize the word that matches their card, give it to them.

    Remind them that nana is another name for grandma.

EXTENDERS

Materials Needed:
1. Playdough in green, pink, yellow and blue.

2. Pattern for house on page 141, scissors, crayons, glue, large sheets of paper.

3. Catalogs that contain people (Sears, J.C. Penneys), scissors, glue, large sheets of paper.

Procedure:
1. To help children understand the relationship of Nana Downstairs (grandma) and Nana Upstairs (great-grandma), have them make clay-people – a green for themselves, pink for mother, yellow for grandma and blue for great-grandma. Explain the relationship – this is you; this is your mother; this is your mother's mother, your grandma; this is your grandma's mother, your mother's grandma, and your great-grandma.

2. Cut out the house pattern. Cut and fold the doors and windows as indicated. Glue the edges of the house to the larger sheet of paper. Open the door and draw a picture of you. Open the downstairs window and draw a picture of Nana Downstairs. Open the upstairs window and draw a picture of Nana Upstairs. Color the house and add flowers and trees if you wish.

3. Cut out pictures to represent people who make up your family or live in your house. Paste to the large sheet of paper. Help children write the names under each and the relationship – sister, mother, friend.

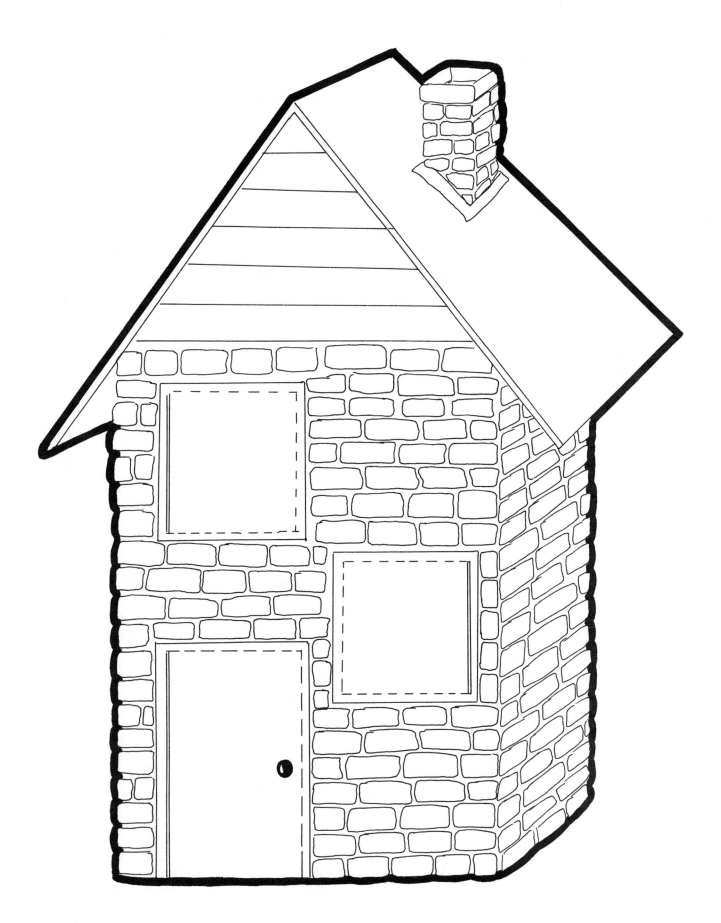

Book 4

ON MOTHER'S LAP
Ann Herbert Scott
(McGraw-Hill, 1972)

A little Eskimo boy named Michael likes to sit in the rocking chair on his mother's lap. One day he sits happily while mother rocks. Then he starts adding things to her lap – a doll, truck, boat, puppy and a blanket. Mother wraps the children and the toys in the reindeer blanket and whispers, "There is always room on mother's lap."

STARTERS

Materials Needed:
1. Classroom toys in a basket, chairs.

2. Paper, pencils, felt marker, scissors.

Procedure:
1. Children sit in chairs in a circle. Pass the toys around. Children take one and put it in their lap.

   Whisper, "Is there still room on your lap?" Continue passing toys, one at a time, until they say their laps are full. Then you add one more tiny item as you whisper, "There is always room on (child's name) lap for one more toy."

2. Cut each child a 3" square of paper. Count the toys on your lap and write the number on the paper. Count the total number of toys on all the laps and write the number on a sheet of paper.

EXTENDERS

Materials Needed:

1. Paper, crayons.

2. Small wooden blocks, pictures from # 1 below.

3. Fun Sheet from page 144, scissors, pencil, stapler.

Procedure:

1. Draw a picture of your family. Write the number of people in one corner.

2. Put the children in groups according to the number of people in their family. Set out the small wooden blocks. Using your picture above, set one block for each person on the paper.

   Math: Which group has the largest number of people in their family. The smallest number? How many groups have more than six? Less than four? Five in their family?

3. Fun Sheet – Cut the pictures apart and arrange them in the correct story sequence. Number the pages and staple together. Use to retell the story.

Book 5

PETER'S CHAIR
Ezra Jack Keats
(Harper, 1967)

Peter's family has a new baby. The baby is in Peter's cradle which has been painted pink. His father is fixing up Peter's high chair and will paint it pink. Peter decides to take his little chair, his baby picture, his dog, cookies and dog biscuits and run away. He sets up his things in front of the house. When he tries to sit in his chair, he discovers he is too big! So Peter moves back inside where he sits in a grown-up chair. Daddy let's him paint his little chair pink for baby Susie.

STARTERS

Materials Needed:

1. Magazines containing baby pictures, scissors, glue, large sheet of butcher paper.

2. Catalogs containing things babies need, scissors, tape, classroom bulletin board.

Procedure:

1. Find out who has babies at home. Discuss ways we can help care for babies.

   Cut out the baby pictures and paste to the butcher paper to make a "baby mural."

2. Discuss "things" babies need. Cut out pictures of things babies need and tape to the bulletin board.

EXTENDERS

Materials Needed:

1. Pink paint, brushes and paper; pink playdough; pink paper and crayons, pink pens, colored pencils and felt markers.

2. Pink styrofoam egg carton, scissors, plastic needles and pink thread.

3. Large, plain cookies, powdered sugar, milk, red food coloring, bowl, spoon, plastic knives for spreading, pink napkins, wax paper.

4. Same as in #1, #2, and #3 except all material is blue.

Procedure:

1. Declare today "a pink day." Use the materials for art activities.

2. Cut the egg cups apart. Cut the carton tops into 1" squares. String the cups and squares alternately and tie the ends of the strings together to make a necklace.

3. Mix powdered sugar and milk to make enough icing for the group. Tint pink. Give each child a piece of wax paper, cookie, knife and napkin. Spread the icing on the cookie. Eat.

4. On the next day, read the book again, substituting the words blue for pink. Declare a "blue day." Repeat all activities.

Book 6

STAYING WITH GRANDMA

Eileen Row

(Bradbury, 1989)

When mommy and daddy go some place where they can't take me along, I stay at grandma's house. At grandma's, I run through the sprinkler, help hang clothes on the line, grandma pushes me in the swing, we catch frogs in the pond, pick vegetables from the garden, take long walks to watch the sunset, and grandma tells me bedtime stories. Staying with grandma means I will have peach jam on toast and, as I pack my things, knowing I will come back soon.

STARTERS

Materials Needed:
1. Classroom chart, felt marker.

2. Classroom chart, felt marker.

Procedure:
1. Ask children what they do when they stay a few days with grandma or other relatives. Write them on the chart.

2. Ask children for suggestions for things to pack when they go to stay a few days with grandma or a relative. List them on the chart.

EXTENDERS

Materials Needed:

1. Chart from #1 above, felt marker.

2. Pages from catalogs that contain children's clothing, scissors, #10 size envelopes, crayons.

3. Pattern – House from page 149, cardboard, large sheets of construction paper, shelf paper, scissors, glue, crayons.

4. Shawl, old eye glasses, apron; man's bow tie and vest.

5. Bread, toaster, peach jam, plastic knives.

Procedure:

1. Review the words on the chart in #1 above. Did the girl in our story do any of these things at her grandma's house? What are some things she did at her grandma's house. Add them to the list.

2. Give each child an envelope. Help them write their name and "suitcase" on the envelope. Cut out pictures of five pieces of clothing you might put in your suitcase for a trip to grandma's house and put them in your envelope. Let children share their items with the class.

3. Make cardboard patterns of the house. Trace around the house onto a large sheet of construction paper. Cut out the house. Fold on dotted lines. Pretend you have a grandma who lives in this house. Open the doors and draw pictures of things you might find inside her house. Glue the center section only of the house to the center of a long piece of shelf paper, close the doors and draw pictures of things you might find outside her house.

4. Have the children lie down to rest. Children can take turns wearing the props (grandma or grandpa) and telling a "bedtime nursery rhyme."

   Place all the dress-up items in the home center to encourage dramatic play.

5. After rest, make toast. Cut the slices in half and spread with peach jam for a snack.

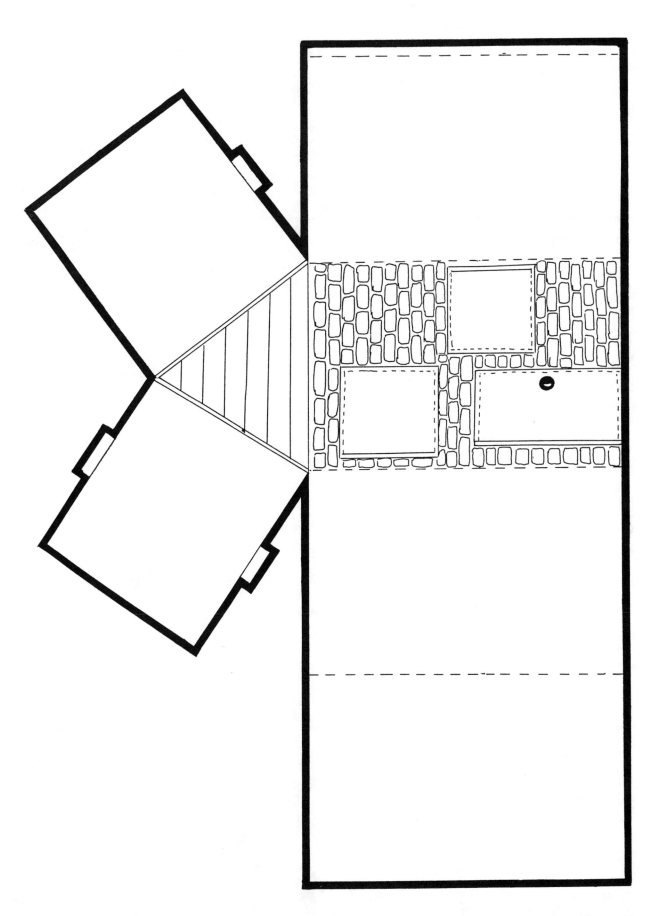

Chapter 8
FRIENDSHIPS

Reading about friendships between children, between animals and between children and animals will help develop an understanding of the importance of friendships and what it means to be a friend.

The Picture Books

Book 1   *Do You Want To Be My Friend?* Eric Carle

Book 2   *Ira Sleeps Over*, Bernard Waber

Book 3   *May I Bring A Friend?*, Beatrice Schenk De Regniers

Book 4   *Play With Me*, Marie Hall Ets

Book 5   *Frog And Toad Together*, Arnold Lobel

Book 6   *Will I Have A Friend?*, Miriam Cohen

DO YOU WANT TO BE MY FRIEND?

Eric Carle

(Crowell, 1971)

This wordless book holds a surprise at each turn of the page as a little mouse looks for a friend. He follows a tail and another and another until he finally finds a (mouse) friend. Part of a long, green snake's tail winds across the bottom of each page.

STARTERS

Materials Needed:

1. Assorted pictures of animals.

2. Pictures of animals with tails, glue, 3 x 5 cards, scissors.

Procedure:

1. Ask, "Do you think animals have friends?" Show the pictures, one at a time, and ask, "Who might be a friend and play with this animal?" Ask why they think so.

2. Prepare ahead of time picture cards of animals without their tails and cards with the animal's tail only.

    Lay out the cards. Choose an animal and then find the card with the matching tail.

EXTENDERS

Materials Needed:

1. Available classroom animals.

2. Cardboard paper towel spools cut into 4" lengths, paint and brushes, safe object for punching holes, heavy yarn, stapler.

3. Mouse ears pattern from page 155, paint and brushes, scissors, glue, stapler, tag board strips 2" x 24".

Procedure:

1. Review the animals mentioned in the story. Go on an animal hunt in the classroom to see how many of the story animals you can find.

2. Snake – paint several spool sections and string them on the yarn. Punch a hole in the front and back spool. Tie the yarn to the spools. Mash one of the end spools and staple shut for snake's head. Paint the features.

3. Paint your mouse ears. Cut out and glue to a headband. Overlap the ends of the headband to fit your head and staple in place.

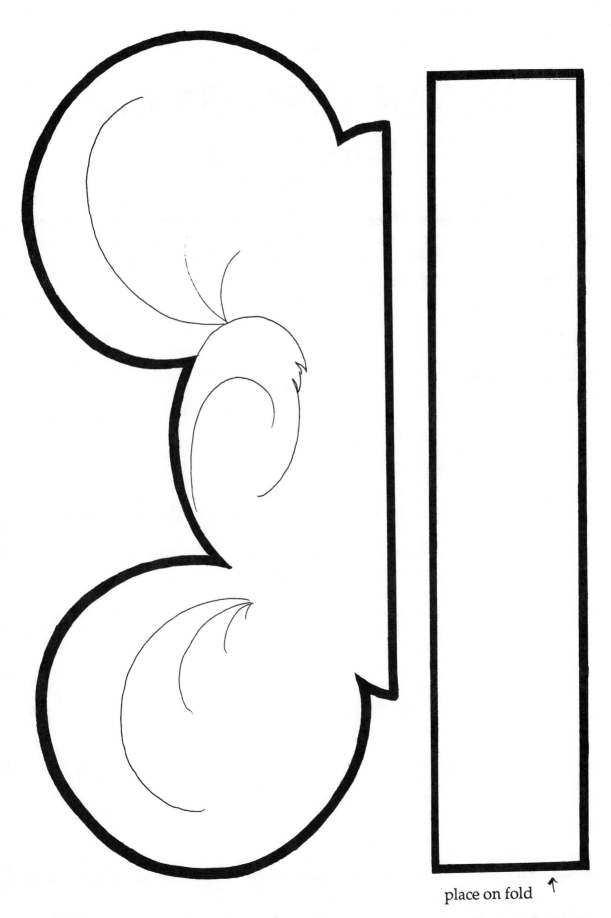

place on fold ↑

IRA SLEEPS OVER

Bernard Wabe

(Houghton Mifflin, 1972)

Upon being invited to a friend's house, Ira has a unique overnight adventure. While packing, his sister asks him if he is going to take his teddy bear. Ira worries, should I? Can I sleep without teddy? He and Reggie have a great time, but when they get ready for bed, Ira gets a happy surprise.

STARTERS

Materials Needed:

1. Paper, crayons.

2. Classroom chart, felt marker.

Procedure:

1. Draw a picture of the favorite toy (or blanket) you like to take to bed.

2. Write each child's name down the chart. As they share their picture, write the name of the item opposite the child's name.

EXTENDERS

Materials Needed:

    1. Pattern from page 158, scissors, crayons, staplers, newspaper.

    2. Action counting rhyme, stuffed teddy bears, yarn.

> **FIVE LITTLE BEARS**
> One little teddy bear with nothing to do.
>   Along comes another, now there are two.
> Two little teddy bears climbing up a tree.
>   Along comes another, now there are three.
> Three little teddy bears, let out a loud roar.
>   Along comes another, now there are four.
> Four little teddy bears, off for a drive.
>   Along comes another, now there are five.

    3. Teddy bears and story listed under # 3 below.

Procedure:

    1. Copy the teddy bear pattern onto heavy, brown construction paper (each child needs two). Draw in the features and then cut out. Staple the two together around the edges, leaving one side open. Tear the newspaper into tiny strips and stuff the bear. Finish stapling.

    2. Divide the class into groups of five. Make a circle of yarn for each group. One child stands in each circle holding their stuffed teddy bear. Recite the rhyme and, when indicated, have another child come to the circle.

    3. Have children act out the following:

> We are going to a sleep-over.
> Get your backpack off the shelf.
> Fill it up with clothes.
> Put your backpack on.
> Put your teddy bear under your arm.
> Walk to your friend's house.
> Lay your teddy bear down. Take off your backpack.
> Take off your clothes. Put on your pajamas.
> Roll out your sleeping bag.
> You and teddy crawl in and go to sleep.

Book 3

MAY I BRING A FRIEND?

Beatrice Schenk De Regniers

(Atheneum, 1974)

In this rhyming story that covers the days of the week, a little girl is invited to have tea with the King and Queen. Being told she can bring a friend sets off a chain of events that ends up with a tea party at the City Zoo.

STARTERS

Materials Needed:

1. Calendar.

2. None.

Procedure:

1. Discuss and help children learn the days of the week. Count together the days of the week, and then the days of the current month. Children take turns counting the number of each day in the month – 4 Sundays, 5 Mondays.

2. Number off 1 through 7 and form groups. Compare the groups to the days of the week. Each group calls off their number and then calls off their day of the week (1, Sunday).

EXTENDERS

Materials Needed:

1. Calendar of the month, numerals 1 through 7 written on white 3 x 5 cards, yarn.

2. Words "first" through "seventh" written on blue 3 x 5 cards.

3. Each day of the week written on 5 x 8 cards, calendar.

4. All cards from above.

5. Patterns from pages 162 & 163, glue in squeeze bottles, colored glitter, scissors.

6. Zoo animal pictures, tea pot of fruit juice, plate with tiny tea cookies, napkins, small cups.

7. Fun Sheet from page 164, scissors, glue.

Procedure:

1. Using the calendar, explain the days of the week as: day one is the first day, day two is the second day, and so on. Go through the cards reviewing – one is first, two is second.

2. Use the yarn to make seven circles in a line. Pass out the blue cards. When you call "first," the child with the card marked 1 will hop to the first circle. When you call "second" the child with the card marked 2 will hop to the second circle, and so on.

3. Use the yarn circles from #2. Pass out the days of the week cards. Call out the days in order and have each child place their card on the appropriate circle.

   Repeat the activity, calling the days out of order.

   Review by pointing to each day and having the children say: Sunday is the first day of the week; Tuesday is the second day of the week, and so on.

4. Mix up the three sets of cards and lay them out face up. Children take turns matching the cards (Sunday, first, and the numeral 1).

5. Copy a crown of your choice onto yellow paper. Make designs by squeezing glue on the crown. Sprinkle glitter into the wet glue. When dry, shake off and save the excess glitter. Overlap the edges of the band and staple to fit your head.

6. Set up the tea-time table. Wear your crown, choose an animal picture to bring to tea.

   Invitation game: Teacher: Judy, please come to tea. Judy: May I bring a friend? Teacher: Yes, please do. Judy: Brent, please come to tea. Brent: May I bring a friend? Judy: Yes, please do, and so on until all are present for tea.

7. Fun Sheet – Cut out the days of the week and the ordinal numbers. Glue the day of the week **above** the correct square, the ordinal **under** the square, and write the number **in** the square.

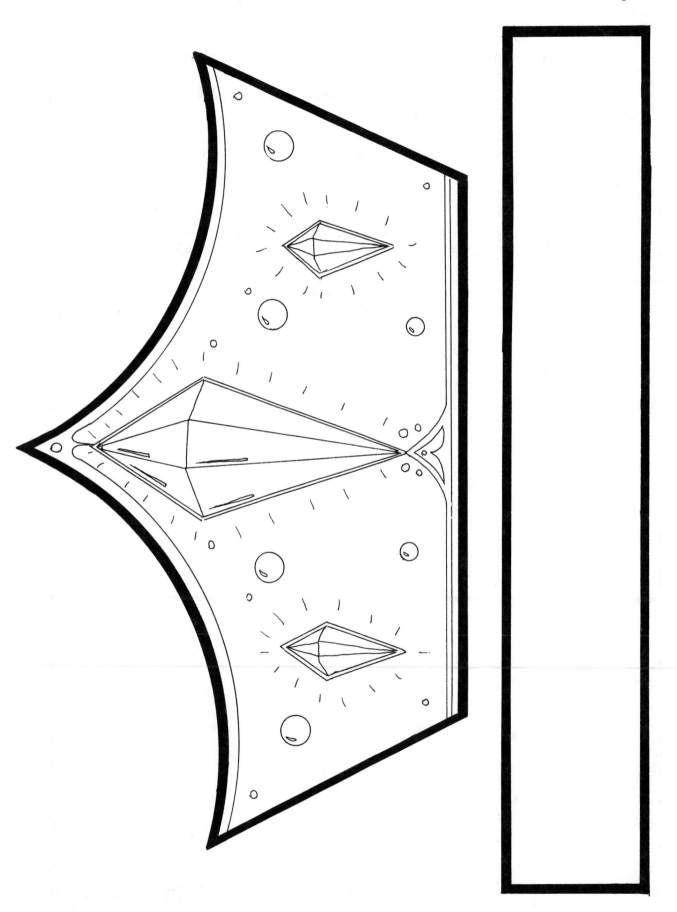

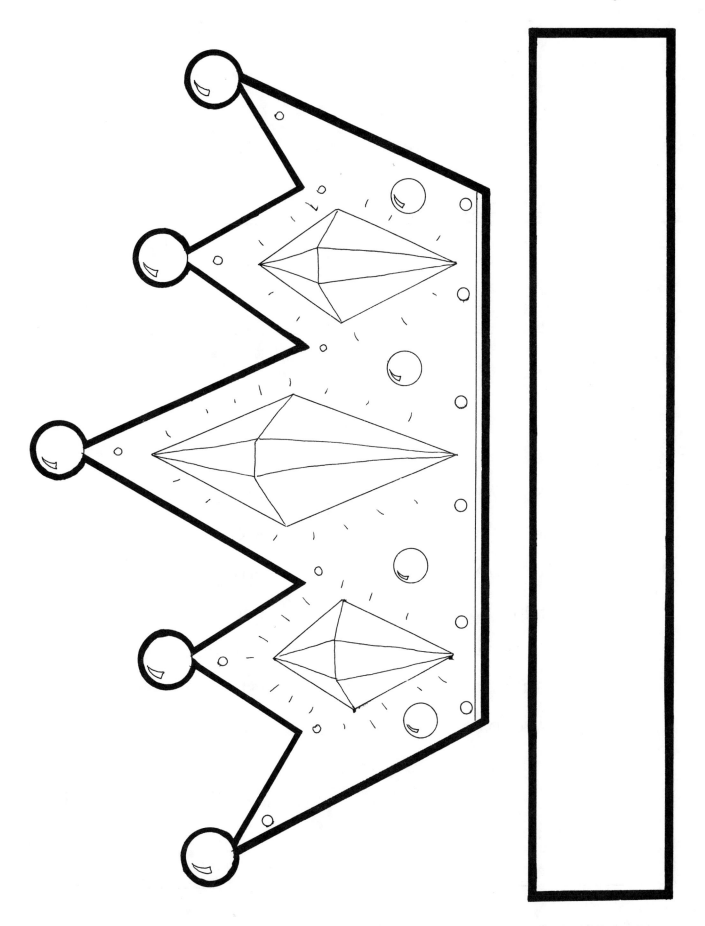

163

Story Sparklers

SUNDAY	FIRST
MONDAY	SECOND
TUESDAY	THIRD
WEDNESDAY	FOURTH
THURSDAY	FIFTH
FRIDAY	SIXTH
SATURDAY	SEVENTH

Book 4

PLAY WITH ME
Marie Hall Ets
(Viking, 1955)

A little girl goes to the meadow looking for a playmate and chases after a grasshopper, frog, turtle, chipmunk, blue jay, rabbit and snake, but they all run away. When she sits down by the pond, not making a sound, the animals slowly come back and join her.

STARTERS

Materials Needed:
1. Picture of a rabbit, turtle and blue jay.

2. Felt marker, 3 x 5 cards.

Procedure:
1. Show the pictures and ask children to show you how they think each animal moves, and where they think each animal might live.

2. Spell out as you print the names of the animals in the story – grasshopper, frog, turtle, chipmunk, blue jay, rabbit, snake – on 3 x 5 cards. Help children learn to recognize the name cards.

EXTENDERS

Materials Needed:
1. Blanket.

2. Yarn, scissors, hole punch, cards from # 2 above.

3. Fun Sheet from page 167, scissors, glue, crayons.

Procedure:
1. Lay out a blanket for the meadow. Each child finds a special place in the room to stand.

   Game: Let's take big hops with the rabbit to the meadow (hop to the blanket). But the rabbit was frightened and hopped back home because the children were too noisy.

   Let's creep on hand and knees with the turtle to the meadow. But the turtle was frightened and crept back home because the children were too noisy.

   Let's fly with the blue jay to the meadow. But the blue jay was frightened and flew back home because the children were too noisy.

   The children sat in the meadow (children come to the blanket). They closed their eyes. They were very quiet and sat so still. Soon the animals came back – the rabbit, the turtle, the blue jay. The animals were tired from hopping and creeping and flying, so they rested in the meadow with the children.

2. Punch 2 holes at the top of the cards. Attach a piece of yarn so the card can be worn around the neck.

   Give each child a card to wear as you play games with the animals, such as "London Bridge" and "Here We Go Around the Mulberry Bush."

3. Fun Sheet – Cut out the animals and glue them to the picture to show where they live in the meadow. Color the picture.

Book 5

FROG AND TOAD TOGETHER

Arnold Lobel

(Harper, 1971)

A collection of five short stories about the friendship of Frog and Toad. Toad likes the flowers that frog grew in his garden. Frog likes the chocolate chip cookies Toad baked. They do things together, solve problems, share and have fun.

STARTERS

Materials Needed:
1. Classroom chart, felt marker, pictures of a frog and a toad.

2. Book cover.

Procedure:
1. Ask children to tell you the difference between a frog and a toad.

    Write frog and toad in two columns at the top of the chart and list the differences:

    Frog: Has smooth skin, lives in water or wet places, has long back legs and is a good jumper, has smaller eyes.

    Toad: Usually has rough, warty skin, is plump and broad, has larger eyes, shorter legs, lives on land, is slow and can not jump as well.

    Glue the frog and toad pictures to the top of the chart.

2. Show the book cover and ask which one is the frog. Why do you think so?

EXTENDERS

Materials Needed:
Read one story at a time followed by one activity.

1. None.

2. Bowl, cotton, radish or grass seed, water.

3. One and a half paper plates for each child, construction paper, scissors, stapler, paint and brushes, glue.

4. None.

5. Fun Sheet from page 170, tagboard, scissors, crayons, glue, #10 size envelopes.

Procedure:
1. Describe toad from the book and have children guess who it is. Describe each child in the class and have children guess who it is. Start with, "Frog and Toad had a friend who . . ."

2. Place the cotton in the bowl. Sprinkle the cotton with seeds. Sing songs to the seeds (like Toad did); recite nursery rhymes. Are our seeds growing? What did Toad's seeds need to make them grow? Set the bowl in a sunny place and keep the cotton wet. In two or three days the seeds will sprout.

3. Fold the plate in half to make a frog face puppet. Staple the half plate to the top of the folded plate to form a hand pocket for opening and closing the mouth. Paint your frog. Cut tongue and eyes from construction paper and glue in place.

4. Play a game of Leap Frog.

5. Fun Sheet puzzle – Glue the picture to a piece of tagboard and then color it. Cut on the dotted lines, mix up the pieces and put the puzzle together. Write "Frog and Toad" and your name on your envelope and use it for keeping your puzzle pieces.

Book 6

WILL I HAVE A FRIEND?

Miriam Cohen

(Macmillan, 1967)

When Jim goes to school for the first time, he worries if he will find a friend. At first he watches. The other kids ignore him and he is unhappy. Finally, at nap time, he finds that he has a new friend!

STARTERS

Materials Needed:
1. None.

2. Strips of white construction paper long enough to fit around a child's wrist and overlap, crayons, tape.

Procedure:
1. Discuss things that friends can do together, and what we could do to make new friends.

2. Make "we're all friends" bracelets by having each child decorate one bracelet. Put all the bracelet strips in a box. Children stand in a circle. The first child draws a bracelet from the box, puts it around the next child's wrist, and tapes the ends together. Continue until each child has a bracelet.

   Hold hands and dance around in a circle singing, "this is the way we dance with our friends" to the tune of the Mulberry Bush.

EXTENDERS

Materials Needed:
1. Paper, crayons and ribbon.

2. None.

3. Rocks about the size of an egg, paint and small brushes, paper bag.

Procedure:
1. Draw a picture, roll it up and tie it with a ribbon. Set up the chairs in a circle, one for each child. Take children outside and let one at a time go inside and place their gift on a chair. Return to the classroom, open the gifts, and call out together "thank-you friend."

2. Assign each child a partner. Take turns being the leader as you two play Follow the Leader.

3. Paint two friendship rocks. Put one in the bag and keep one. Children take turns drawing a friendship rock from the bag.

Chapter 9
CONCEPTS

The following picture books will help young children discover everyday concepts. Story related math activities and art projects, as well as movement and other physical means of involvement, will reinforce their understanding of these basic ideas.

The Picture Books

Book 1   *All About Opposites*, Ruth Thompson

Book 2   *A Picture For Harold's Room*, Crockett Johnson

Book 3   *Little Blue And Little Yellow*, Leo Lionni

Book 4   *The Little Red House*, Norma Jean Sawicki

Book 5   *Over In The Meadow*, Olive A. Wadsworth

Book 6   *Shapes*, John Reiss

ALL ABOUT OPPOSITES
Ruth Thomson
(Garth Stevens, 1987)

Roy's rabbit and friend discover concepts dealing with opposites. Good pictures that include big/little; up/down; open/shut; hot/cold.

STARTERS

Materials Needed:
1. None.

2. Large shoe box, 12" lengths of red and blue yarn.

Procedure:
1. Divide the class into two groups and have them stand in a line back to back. Ask if both groups are facing the same direction. Explain that the groups are facing opposite directions.

2. Turn the shoe box on its side and place it in the middle of the room. Give half the group red yarn and the other half blue. Give opposite directions to two children from each group such as, place the red yarn over the box; place the blue yarn under the box. Repeat using the following concepts: on/off; in/out; behind/in front; right side/left side; by the long/short side of the box.

EXTENDERS

Materials Needed:

1. None.

2. Yarn.

3. Yellow and blue paper plates.

4. Set out materials to demonstrate the following concepts: soft/hard; smooth/rough; wet/dry; hot/cold; open/shut; big/little; tall/short; in/out.

Procedure:

1. Give a direction for bodily movement and then have children take turns giving directions to the group for the opposite movement – stand up/sit down, slide forward/slide backward, move your hand up/move your hand down, step forward/step backward, run in place fast/run in place slow.

2. Use the yarn to make a large circle on the floor. Children can take turns giving opposite directions such as: Tiptoe on the yarn, tiptoe off the yarn, jump in the circle/out, move forward on the yarn/move backward.

3. Give each child a paper plate. Hold the plate with both hands. Move the plate over your head/under your feet; in front of your knees/in back of your knees; up high/down low; fast/slow.

   Give each child a blue and a yellow paper plate. Hold one plate in each hand. Give verbal directions for placement of the yellow plate. Then they are to do the opposite with the blue plate such as: Yellow plate up (they must also move the blue plate down).

4. Have children match the opposites.

Book 2

A PICTURE FOR HAROLD'S ROOM

Crockett Johnson

(Scholastic, 1960)

Harold wants a picture for his room. He takes a purple crayon and draws buildings until he has a town. Then he draws hills, clouds, the sea, a fish, boat, rocks, a lighthouse, mountains and even a train track. Harold keeps drawing until he ends up back in his room and there he draws a picture for the wall.

STARTERS

Materials Needed:

1. Two glasses half filled with water, red and blue food coloring.

2. Powdered red and blue tempera paint, individual containers for mixing paint, plastic spoons, water.

Procedure:

1. Squeeze 10 drops of red food coloring into one glass and 10 drops of blue into the other. Observe and discuss the results. Pour the red water into the other glass. Discuss the observations.

2. Mix water with the blue paint to make a thin paste. Slowly stir in red paint until the mixtures become thick and turns purple.

EXTENDERS

Materials Needed:
1. Felt marker, assorted shades of purple paper.

2. Water frozen in a half-gallon milk carton, large pan, red and blue food coloring in squeeze bottles.

3. Purple finger paint from above, large sheets of finger paint paper.

Procedure:
1. Collect purple items from the classroom. Compare the different shades.

   Set out the purple paper. Ask children for other names for shades of purple – lavender, lilac, violet, orchid. Write the color word on the paper that they feel best describes it.

   Place the purple items on the matching paper.

2. Remove ice from the milk carton and place in the pan. Have children first predict, and then see what will happen when we squeeze drops of red and blue food coloring on top of the block of ice.

3. Cover your paper with finger paint. Reread portions of the story that children can easily draw into the paint such as Harold drew a house, tree, flowers, clouds. Let children finish their picture for Harold's room as they wish.

Book 3

LITTLE BLUE AND LITTLE YELLOW

Leo Lionni

(Astor, 1959)

Little Blue has many friends (colors), but his best friend is Little Yellow who lives across the street. They like to play games together. One day Little Blue felt sad because he thought his friend was lost. When he found Little Yellow, they hugged and hugged until they were green.

STARTERS

Materials Needed:
1. None.

2. None.

Procedure:
1. Call out colors at random. Have children hold up their hand if they are wearing that color.

   Have children stand if they are wearing blue; yellow; green; any other color.

2. Have each child find an object in the classroom that is their favorite color. Sort the colors to find the most popular color. Set the yellow and blue items in front of you as you begin the story.

EXTENDERS

Materials Needed:

1. Liquid laundry starch, powdered blue and yellow paint, finger paint paper.

2. A small ball of blue and yellow playdough for each child.

3. Large coffee filters, blue and yellow food color in squeeze bottles.

Procedure:

1. Pour two circles of starch on the paper. Sprinkle one color of paint into each circle of starch. Mix the two separately and then mix together to form green. Make designs in the paint. Let dry.

2. Mix and knead the two colors of playdough together to form green. What can you make with your green playdough?

3. Fold your coffee filter several times. Squeeze drops of blue and yellow food color onto the filter. Unfold the filter and let dry. How many different colors or shades did you make?

Book 4

THE LITTLE RED HOUSE

Norma Jean Sawicki

(Lothrop, 1989)

There was a little red house. In the little red house was a little green house and so the story continues incorporating nine colors. Inside the last box, was YOU!

STARTERS

Materials Needed:

1. Large sheets of paper, crayons.

2. Large assortment of broken crayons with the paper removed, picture from #1 below.

Procedure:

1. Draw a picture of a house.

2. Pretend you are going to paint your house. Choose a color and using the side of the crayon, follow along the outside of your house to make another house.

EXTENDERS

Materials Needed:

1. A small doll hidden in a paper bag tied with a ribbon, yarn in 9 different colors.

2. Large cardboard box with lid removed.

3. Fun Sheet from page 183, crayons, scissors.

Procedure:

1. Tell the children there is someone in this bag who needs a house. Work together to outline a very large house with yarn. Tell the children it is not right for our friend, they need to make another. Continue outlining houses, one inside the other, until you have nine houses – one that is just right for our friend. Remove the doll from the bag and place it in the last house.

2. Children take turns squatting inside the box as the others chant this rhyme:

> Someone's in the box, I wonder who?
> Is it an animal that lives in the zoo?
> A turtle, a frog, who could it be?
> Who is in the box?
> (a child in the box jumps up and answers loudly)
> It's (Sally), it's me!

3. Copy the Fun Sheet onto heavy, white, construction paper. Color each section a different color. Draw a picture of "you" in the last house. Cut out the largest house. Fold forward on the center dotted line. Unfold and cut the houses apart. Houses should stand.

Use cut-out houses to tell the story of "The Little Red House."

Use your house pieces for a puzzle.

Book 5

OVER IN THE MEADOW

Olive A. Wadsworth

(Scholastic, 1971)

A counting book about ten different animals that live in the meadow. One at a time the mother animals give instructions to their little ones, and the baby animals obey.

STARTERS

Materials Needed:

1. Blocks, tiles, spools and other classroom items that can be grouped.

2. Groups of items from #1 below, set of 3 x 5 cards numbered one through ten.

Procedure:

1. Have children put the items into groups so there is one item, and then groups of 2, 3, 4, on up to 10.

2. Have children place the matching cards by the "groups."

   Have the children form into groups (one group at a time) that matches they toy groups. Let each group do something together (as the animals did in the story), such as clap, stamp, hop.

EXTENDERS

Materials Needed:
1. None.

2. Playdough, plastic drinking straws.

3. Cards used in #2 above.

4. Patterns from pages 186 & 187, glue, scissors, crayons, wooden craft sticks.

5. Animal stick puppets made in #3 below.

Procedure:
1. Review the "groups" from #1 in Starter section.

2. Make a playdough birthday cake. Cut the straws into candle lengths. Give each child 12 candles.

   Count one to ten as you add candles. How many candles are left over?

   Put the of candles on your cake to show how old you are.

   Use the candles for addition and subtraction activities.

3. Lay the cards on the table. Call out the animals from the story and let children take turns finding the matching card number (one little turtle, two little fish).

4. Color and cut out the ten animal pictures. Glue an animal to the top of each stick to use as a stick puppet.

   Children use their puppet to count and act out the story as you read it again.

5. Reread the book (left sides of pages only) omitting the number. Have children hold up the matching animal puppet and say the rhyming number. (Over in the meadow, where the stream runs blue, lived an old mother fish and her little fishes _____ (two).

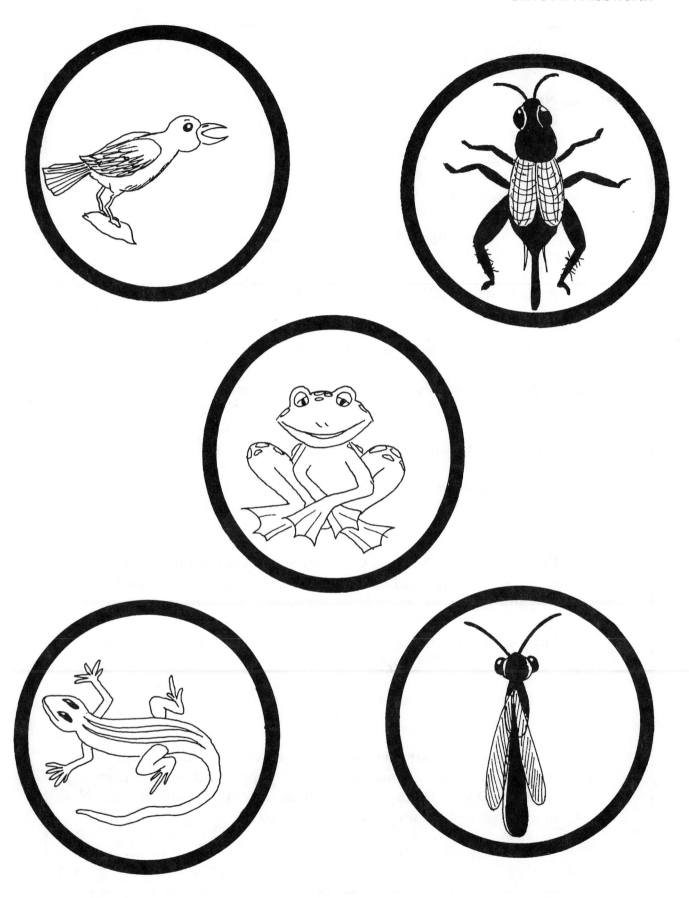

Book 6

SHAPES

John Reiss

(Bradbury, 1974)

The author introduces the basic shapes along with matching familiar objects. Oval, pyramid, sphere and cube are also included. The book ends by bringing the shapes together for a "circus of shapes" and a party.

STARTERS

Materials Needed:

1. Shape crackers, 2 for each child, in a flat plate.

2. Crackers from #1, classroom objects, juice, cups.

Procedure:

1. Have each child choose a cracker and identify the shape. Discuss similarities and differences in the shapes.

2. Find something in the classroom that is the same shape as your cracker. Choose another cracker that is different from the one you have. Have crackers and juice for snack.

EXTENDERS

Materials Needed:
1. Thick fingerpaint, paper.

2. Construction paper cut into geometric shapes, glue, large sheets of paper.

3. Round, plastic lids in several sizes, crayons, large sheets of paper.

4. Yarn.

Procedure:
1. Have children practice drawing shapes in the paint.

   Name a shape and have children draw it.

   Give directions such as: Draw a circle at the top of the paper; draw a triangle in one corner of the paper.

2. Glue the cut-out shapes to the paper to form your own circus of shapes.

3. Trace around the lids to form animals, snowman, or other creative designs.

4. Use the yarn to form shape outlines on the floor.

Chapter 10
HOLIDAYS

These books and related activities will help you extend your holiday celebrations by giving you fresh ideas to stretch your favorite holiday through fun activities as well as suggestions for other holidays that are often overlooked.

The Picture Books

Book 1   *A Garden For Groundhog*, Lorna Balian

Book 2   *Easter Parade*, Mary Chalmers

Book 3   *Happy Birthday, Dear Duck*, Eve Bunting

Book 4   *Jeremy Bean's St. Patrick's Day*, Alice Schertle

Book 5   *The Mother's Day Mice*, Eve Bunting

Book 6   *The Valentine Bears*, Eve Bunting

A GARDEN FOR GROUNDHOG

Lorna Balian

(Abingdon, 1985)

Mr. and Mrs. O'Leary lived on a farm. Groundhog lived there too. Every year the O'Learys planted a garden, but Groundhog would eat their vegetables. This year they grew too much zucchini. The following year, the O'Learys try to trick Groundhog, but since groundhogs can not read they ended up with more zucchini. A good explanation of Groundhog Day is woven into the story.

STARTERS

Materials Needed:
1. Zucchini squash, classroom chart, felt markers, plastic knives, small paper plates.

2. Flashlights.

Procedure:
1. Set out the zucchini and write the word on the chart. Give two or three children a squash to divide equally between them. Then instruct them to cut from their portion a circle, square, rectangle and a triangle. Taste the zucchini and discuss the taste and texture. Ask for ways zucchini can be used in recipes – cake, bread – and add to the chart.

2. Let children experiment with the flashlight to make shadows on the wall.

EXTENDERS

Materials Needed:

1. Chart from #1 above, felt marker.

2. Groundhog pattern from page 195, large styrofoam drinking cups, plastic straws, crayons, felt markers, glue, scissors, stapler.

3. Lengths of yarn, large, gray paper cloud, smaller yellow paper sun.

4. Fun Sheet from page 196, scissors, crayons, glue.

Procedure:

1. Review the ways Mrs. O'Leary served zucchini and add them to your chart.

2. Color and cut out the groundhog patterns, glue them back to back, and staple to the top of the straw. Use the felt markers to decorate Groundhog's hole (cup). Punch a hole in the bottom of the cup to fit the straw. Push the straw up to move Groundhog out of his hole to look for his shadow. Pull the straw down to move Groundhog back into his hole.

3. Each child makes a groundhog hole with yarn and squats inside the yarn circle. Hold up the paper sun and have children act out what the groundhog did in the story (goes back to sleep).

   Then place the cloud over the sun and repeat. Now pretend to plant a garden for Groundhog.

4. Cut out the word boxes from the Fun Sheet and glue them opposite the matching vegetable. Color the vegetables. Draw a picture of Groundhog's face by the vegetable that was planted for him.

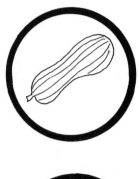

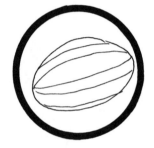

tomato	bean	onion	melon
zucchini	potato	pea (pod)	

Book 2

EASTER PARADE

Mary Chalmers

(Harper, 1988)

It's time for the annual Easter Parade! Easter Chicken comes from the mountains, Easter Rabbit comes from the woods and Easter Duck comes from the lake. They all meet at Easter Farm, load up their cart and parade down the road making their deliveries to all the little rabbits, possums, mice, kittens, and even the ladybugs. The three Easter animals say good-by and each returns home until next spring.

STARTERS

Materials Needed:
1. Pictures of parades.

2. Toy chicken, rabbit and duck and several other animals concealed in a paper bag.

Procedure:
1. Show the parade pictures and have children tell you about them. Discuss kinds of parades and parades children have attended.

2. Have children take turns drawing an animal from the bag and identifying it. After each draw ask, "Is this an Easter animal?" Set the chicken, rabbit and duck in front of you as you read the story.

EXTENDERS

Materials Needed:

1. Patterns from page 199, 2" wide tagboard strips to fit around child's head, scissors, stapler, glue, cotton balls and craft feather.

2. Headbands made in #1 below.

3. Pattern from page 200, heavy white paper, dyed egg shells, plastic bags, liquid glue, scissors.

Procedure:

1. Children choose one of the animal patterns to cut out and glue to the front of the tagboard strip. Add feathers or cotton. Overlap the ends of the headband to fit your head and staple together.

   Wear the headbands and march around the room clapping hands or playing rhythm instruments for an animal Easter parade.

2. For creative movement, wear the headbands from #1 above. Assign parts of the room to be mountains, woods, and lake. Stand in center of room and call the chickens to climb down from the mountain; rabbits to hop out of the woods; ducks to swim out from the lake. Next have them all climb; then hop; and then swim. Play "Ring Around the Rosy." Then instruct chickens to climb back to the mountain; rabbits to hop back to the woods; ducks to swim back to the lake; and all rest.

3. Copy the egg pattern onto heavy paper and cut out. Crush egg shell in the plastic bags. Cover the egg with glue and sprinkle with crushed egg shells.

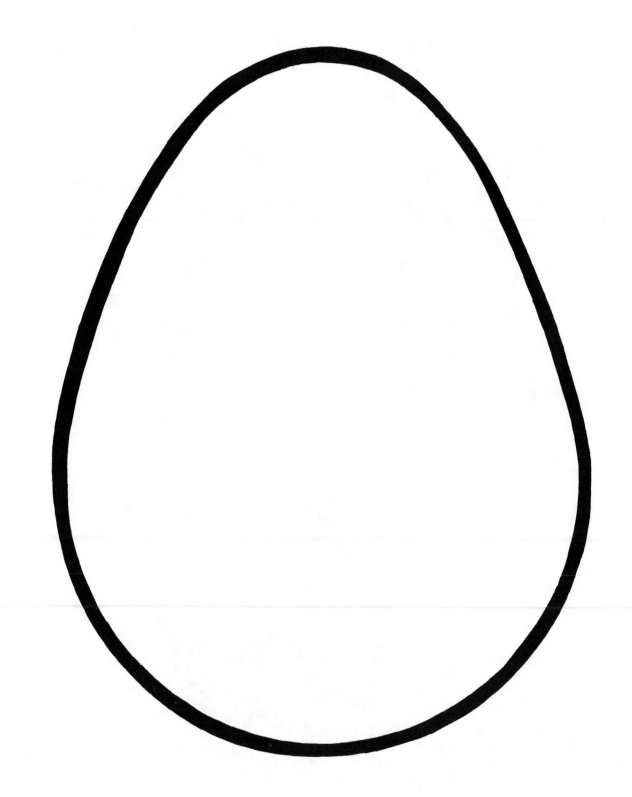

Book 3

HAPPY BIRTHDAY, DEAR DUCK

Eve Bunting

(Clarion, 1988)

For his birthday, Duck's animal friends give him a swim suit, green hat, fat, yellow chair, fishing pole, diving board and slide, sunglasses, ball, scuba mask and suntan oil. But Duck lives in the desert, not near the lake or sea. Tortoise came late and brought just the present they needed to have a great party – an inflatable plastic pool and it was big enough for all!

STARTERS

Materials Needed:

1. None.

2. Bring in as many of the items listed in the story as possible.

Procedure:

1. Hum Happy Birthday. Have children identify the song and then hum it with you.

2. Set out and identify the items, but keep the pool hidden. Bring out the pool after you read the story.

EXTENDERS

Materials Needed:
1. A small margarine tub for each child, decorating material from your "good junk" box, playdough.

2. Small paper bags, long pieces of ribbon or yarn.

3. Birthday cakes and gifts from #1 and #2 below, toy duck, plastic pool, cookies.

4. Patterns from pages 203 & 204, crayons, scissors, glue, blue paper plates.

Procedure:
1. Make a birthday cake by inverting the margarine tub and covering it with a thin flat sheet of playdough. Press bits of decorating material into the playdough.

2. Give each child a small paper bag and a long ribbon. They are to secretly select a small toy from the classroom, place it in the bag and twist and tie the top with ribbon.

3. It is time for Duck's birthday party. Place duck in pool. Children bring their cakes and gifts and sit in or around the pool. Sing "Happy Birthday Dear Duck," and serve the cookies. Have children take turns untying their bag and describing the toy for others to guess.

4. Color, cut out and paste duck's birthday gifts to the paper plate pool.

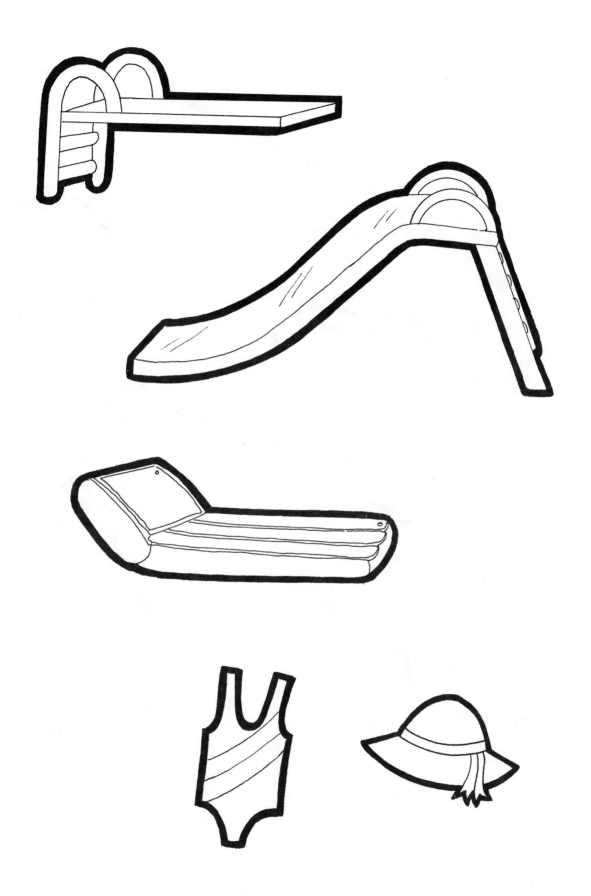

Book 4

JEREMY BEAN'S ST. PATRICK'S DAY

Alice Schertle

(Lothrop, 1987)

Jeremy's class is planning a celebration for St. Patrick's Day, and of course everyone is wearing green. Jeremy planned to wear his green sweater, but he forgot. How can he face his classmates? Jeremy makes a new friend, the principal, who helps make it the best St. Patrick's Day ever by loaning Jeremy his green bow tie.

STARTERS

Materials Needed:
1. Four nested boxes (paper bags can be used), patterns from page 207, several different shades of green paper, scissors, glue, 3 x 5 cards.

2. All the sets of cards made in #1 below.

Procedure:
1. Before class trace a snake, hat, bow tie and shamrock onto each shade of green paper. Cut out and glue each to a 3 x 5 card. Using one set of cards, place one card in each box (shamrock card in last box).

   Show the large box (which contains the other boxes and cards). "There is a picture of something green in this box," (open the box and show snake card). Repeat as you open each box. Make no comments as children guess until the last box. Then ask what they think we will find in the box. Open the last box.

   Recognize green clothing worn by children. Discuss St. Patrick's Day explaining that green became a symbol for St. Patrick's Day because of the green hills, valleys and shamrocks that grow in Ireland.

2. Give each child a shamrock card in a different shade. Place the remaining cards upside down on the table. Children take turns turning over one card at each turn until they find their four matching shade cards.

EXTENDERS

Materials needed:

1. Patterns from page 208, and from #1 above, scissors, paper plates, green construction paper, green yarn, hole punch.

2. Patterns from #1 above, pattern from page 209, white shelf paper (cut into placemat size), green paper, scissors, glue, paper clips, green napkins, green fruit drink, cups, green apples, plastic knives. Ask parents to provide shamrock shape cookies with green icing.

Procedure:

1. Trace the large shamrock onto the paper plate and cut out. Trace other symbols from green paper and glue to the inverted plate hat. Punch holes on opposite sides of the hat and attach pieces of yarn long enough to tie under your chin.

2. Cut bow ties and ribbon ties from green paper and attach to clothing with a paper clip.

   Cut the holiday symbols from green paper and glue to the white paper to make a placemat.

   Have children prepare the apples and cut into serving pieces. Have a St. Patrick's party. Wear hats and ties and serve apples, juice and cookies.

Book 5

THE MOTHER'S DAY MICE

Eve Bunting

(Clarion, 1986)

Biggest mouse, middle mouse and little mouse live at the edge of the strawberry patch. Early one morning the three mice set out to find surprise gifts for their mother. Biggest mouse and middle mouse find their surprises. Little mouse wanted honeysuckle that grew only at Honeysuckle Cottage, but there was a big cat sitting on the porch. Then something inside the cottage gives him an idea. The mice run home. Little mouse is last to give his Mother's Day surprise – he claps his hands and begins to sing a Mother's Day song and everyone joins in.

STARTERS

Materials Needed:
1. None.

2. Pictures cut from catalogs or newspaper ads showing both suitable and unsuitable Mother's Day gifts.

Procedure:
1. Sing "Hickory Dickory Dock." Clap out the rhythm; tap out the rhythm by tapping your toe on the floor; tapping your finger on the table.

   Repeat using Happy Mother's Day to the tune of "Happy Birthday"

2. Lay the pictures on the floor. Children take turns selecting one that would be a good Mother's Day gift. Decide who in the family would like the other items for a gift.

EXTENDERS

Materials Needed:
1. Patterns from page 212, crayons, scissors, yellow paper plates, glue, wooden tongue depressors.

2. Styrofoam balls in 2 sizes, colored tooth picks, knife for teacher use, brown construction paper.

Procedure:
1. To make a fan, color, cut out and glue the 3 mice to the inside of the paper plate. Glue the top half of the wooden tongue depressor to the back of the plate.

2. Stack the two balls and secure with tooth picks to make a mouse. Slice off the bottom of the larger ball so the mouse stands. Cut ears from paper and attach with toothpicks. Use broken toothpicks to make facial features.

Book 6

THE VALENTINE BEARS

Eve Bunting

(Clarion, 1983)

On October 14th, Mr. and Mrs. Bear settle in for the winter. Four months later the alarm wakes Mrs. Bear. While Mr. Bear continues to sleep, she gathers up her hidden gifts – the honey pot, crunchy dried beetles and bugs, and two valentine poems – and then she tries to wake Mr. Bear. Finally she tosses a can of water on him. Mr Bear jumps up and surprises her with a box of her favorite chocolate covered ants.

STARTERS

Materials Needed:

1. None.

2. None.

3. Recording of "Teddy Bear's Picnic."

Procedure:

1. Lead children in the following bear related activities.

   Song: The Bear Went Over the Mountain
   Action rhyme: Teddy Bear, Teddy Bear, Turn Around

2. Discuss animals that hibernate – bears, frogs, chipmunks, snakes and bats. The World Book Encyclopedia is a good resource.

3. Play the recording of "Teddy Bear's Picnic" and have a quiet listening time.

EXTENDERS

Materials Needed:

1. Heart stickers in five sizes, styrofoam cups in five sizes that will fit one inside the other, red and pink felt markers.

2. Pattern from page 215, scissors, crayons, wooden tongue depressors, glue.

3. Pattern from page 216, scissors, crayons.

Procedure:

1. Give each child one cup in each size to decorate on the outside. On the inside bottom, glue heart stickers in graduated sizes small to large. Invert the cups and glue one small heart sticker to the bottom of the largest cup. Add 2 hearts to the next, then 3, 4, and 5.

   Valentine cups can be stacked one inside the other, and inverted and stacked. They can also be set out in order largest to smallest and smallest to largest.

   Use the cups for counting; finding largest and smallest (heart and cup); finding the cup with 3 hearts.

2. Decorate and cut out the bear face mask. Cut out the eye sections. Glue the bottom part of the mask to the top of the tongue depressor to make a face mask.

3. Cut out the hearts. Color the "I, heart and U." Turn over and decorate the back of each heart. Fold on dotted lines. Open the hearts and read the message (I love you).

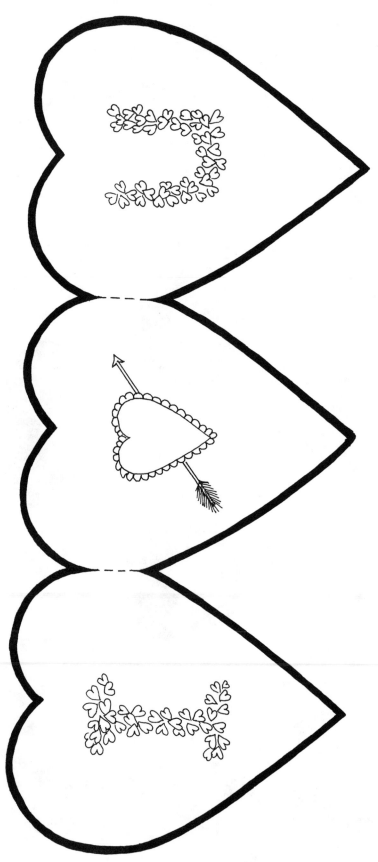

Chapter 11
CLASSICS

As children discover these books, some having been read by two previous generations, they will be introduced to animals and people, each presented with a problem that they must solve. The activities will stretch their imagination and challenge their conceptual abilities.

The Picture Books

Book 1   *Ask Mr. Bear*, Marjorie Flack

Book 2   *Caps For Sale*, Esphyr Slobodkina

Book 3   *Corduroy*, Don Freeman

Book 4   *Curious George Learns The Alphabet*, H.A. Rey

Book 5   *Make Way For Ducklings*, Robert McCloskey

Book 6   *Where The Wilds Things Are*, Maurice Sendak

ASK MR. BEAR
Marjorie Flack
(MacMillan, 1932)

What to give his mother for her birthday poses a problem for Danny. His friends, Chicken, Goose, Goat, Sheep and Cow all offer suggestions, but they are for things she already has. Then he finds Bear who whispers something in his ear and now he knows just what his gift for mother will be. Mother gets a surprise – a big birthday bear hug!

STARTERS

Materials Needed:
   1. None.

   2. Classroom chart, felt marker.

Procedure:
   1. Play the "whisper game." Have children sit in a circle. Whisper in the first child's ear, "Ask Mr. Bear." Each child whispers what they hear into the next child's ear. The last child tells what he hears.

   2. Write children's suggestions for good birthday gifts for mothers on the chart.

EXTENDERS

Materials Needed:

1. Patterns from page 221, scissors, crayons, glue, wooden craft sticks, #10 white envelopes.

2. None.

Procedure:

1. Color, cut out and then glue the pictures to craft sticks to make stick puppets. Decorate the envelope for storing the puppets.

   Reread the story and have children hold up each puppet as it is mentioned in the story and then lay the puppets out in order, one following the other.

2. Children stand in line one behind the other. Whisper "skip" into the leaders ear. The leader calls out "skip." Everyone skips as they count ten skips. The leader goes to the end of the line and you whisper "hop" into the next leader's ear. Continue with gallop, then trot (used in the story). Repeat until everyone has a turn as the leader.

Book 2

CAPS FOR SALE

Esphyr Slobodkina

(Addison-Wesley, 1940)

A tale of a peddler who sells caps, some monkeys who steal his caps while he sleeps, and how the man tricks the monkeys and gets his hats back.

The peddler wears a checked cap. On top of his cap, he balances four hats in each color – brown, white, grey, red – in this order.

STARTERS

Materials Needed:

1. Collection of hats or pictures of hats.

2. Seventeen classroom blocks or objects that can be stacked.

Procedure:

1. Set out the hats, one at a time, and have children identify the wearer. Compare the differences. Sort the hats by color and count the number in each group.

2. Count the blocks together, stack them and count again.

   Discuss the need to balance each block to make the stack.

EXTENDERS

Materials Needed:
1. None.

2. Patterns from page 224, scissors, brown, white, gray and red construction paper, crayons.

Procedure:
1. Stand in a circle. Say to the children, "Give me back my caps," and clap your hands. Children mimic your movements. Then children take turns doing "their own thing" to be mimicked by the group.

2. Cut one cap, in each size, from each color of paper (16 caps; younger children make one cap in each color – 4). Cut another large white cap and use the crayons to make the peddler's checked cap.

   Use the caps for math activities such as: Count the caps. If you sold each cap for one-cent how much money would you make? Each cap for two-cents (count by 2's); each cap for five-cents (count by 5's). If you sold half of you caps, how many would you have left?

   Sort the caps by color. Stack each color by size, largest to smallest. Stack the stacks in this order – brown, white, gray, red.

   Place the checked cap on your head and add the stack of caps. Balancing the caps on your head: walk slowly; walk fast; walk backwards; sit down with your back against the wall; stand up.

   Walk while balancing one cap on your shoulder; on your elbow; on the back of your hand. Hop while balancing one cap on your knee; on your toe.

Book 3

CORDUROY

Don Freeman

(Viking, 1968)

Corduroy, a toy bear, lives in a department store. No one wants to buy Corduroy who has lost the button from the shoulder strap of his green overalls. One night he sets out to find the lost button, but the night watchman finds him and puts him back on his shelf. The next day a little girl comes in, buys him, takes him home and sews a new button on his shoulder strap.

STARTERS

Materials Needed:

1. Piece of corduroy fabric.

2. An assortment of buttons including plastic, wooden, cloth covered, leather.

3. Child's corduroy overalls with shoulder straps and missing button (or another item of clothing), button collection from above and the missing button, needle and thread.

Procedure:

1. Let children feel the corduroy fabric and describe how it looks and feels.

2. Sort the buttons by color. Then ask for other ways we could sort the buttons – size, texture.

3. Show the strap with the missing button. Let children help you find the missing button from the collection and then watch you sew it on. Discuss other kinds of fasteners, hooks, snaps, zippers.

EXTENDERS

Materials Needed:

1. Collection of buttons from #2 above, old socks in different colors.

2. A piece of corduroy and several other textured fabrics, paper bag.

3. Strips of fabric about 12" x 3", plastic needles, thread, buttons, scissors.

Procedure:

1. Make "feeling socks" by filling soxs with buttons as follows: Four buttons of different shapes (find the oval one); four in different sizes (find the smallest one); five buttons, two alike (find two alike); five in different textures (find the rough one).

2. Place the fabric pieces in the bag. Children each take a turn feeling and finding the piece of corduroy.

3. Help children sew a button of their choice on one end of the fabric strip. Cut a hole in the other end to fit the button.

Book 4

CURIOUS GEORGE LEARNS THE ALPHABET

H.A. Rey
(Houghton Mifflin, 1963)

The man with the yellow hat helps George learn his alphabet by drawing pictures around each letter. Both upper and lower case letters are included. George uses the doughnuts he bought for a snack to spell out words.

STARTERS

Materials Needed:
1. Cheerios cereal.

2. Long sheet of shelf paper, felt marker, paper bag, individual, commercial type letters of the alphabet (or cut your own or draw them on cards).

Procedure:
1. Have children sit in a circle with their hands cupped behind them. Drop a Cheerio in each child's hand. Let them feel it and name things that are the same shape.

2. Have children repeat the alphabet slowly as you draw the letters in a long line on the paper. Place the individual letters in the bag. Children take turns drawing a letter from the bag, identifying it, and placing it on top of the matching letter on the paper.

EXTENDERS

Materials Needed:

1. Playdough.

2. Cheerios, wax paper.

3. Pattern from page 229, scissors, hole punch, paper fasteners (brads), brown paper, crayons, yarn.

Procedure:

1. Roll the playdough into a "snake" and form the letter "O." Make other letters from the playdough.

2. Use Cheerios to spell out your name on the wax paper. Eat your name!

3. Trace the monkey pattern on brown paper. Draw in the features and cut out. Punch holes as indicated. Assemble the monkey by fastening with paper brads. Tie a loop of yarn through the head hole.

Book 5

MAKE WAY FOR DUCKLINGS

Robert McCloskey

(Viking, 1941)

While looking for a place to live and raise their young, Mr. and Mrs. Mallard (ducks) arrive in Boston. They build their nest on the pond in the park and hatch eight ducklings. Living in the park turns into quite an adventure and the Mallards decide to make the little island in the park their permanent home.

STARTERS

Materials Needed:

1. Dish pan of water, 2 plastic ducks wrapped in paper.

2. Eight plastic ducklings, or other floating items to represent ducklings, wrapped in paper.

Procedure:

1. Slowly unwrap the ducks and float them on the water. Discuss ducks, where they live and what they eat.

2. Unwrap the ducklings. Give each child a duck to float on the "pond."

EXTENDERS

Materials Needed:
1. Duck family and pan of water from #1 and #2 above.

2. Materials for making a nest – torn paper, bits of string or yarn, scraps of paper, packing material, straw, liquid glue, pieces of cardboard, duck pattern from page 232, scissors, construction paper.

Procedure:
1. Ask how many ducklings there were in the story and how many ducks in the Mallard family.

   Ask how many ducklings there are in our pond and how many ducks are in our duck family.

   Use the ducks for math activities such as: Have a child take away three ducks – how many ducks are on the pond? One duck swims back (return duck to pond) how many ducks are on our pond?

2. Glue a layer of nest material to the cardboard to make a duck nest. Add more glue and another layer of materials. Trace the duck pattern onto construction paper. Cut out, fold on the dotted line, and place on the nest.

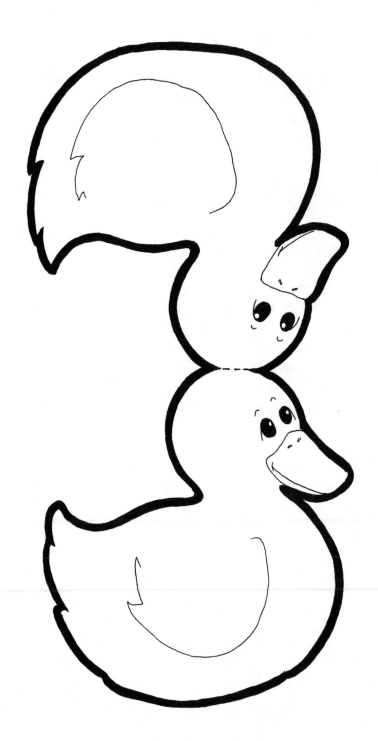

Book 6

WHERE THE WILD THINGS ARE

Maurice Sendak

(Harper, 1963)

Mischievous Max is sent to his room without any supper. Through Max's imagination, a forest grows in his room, an ocean appears, and Max climbs into his private boat and sails off to where the wild things live. The strange animals crown him king and the great rumpus begins. Max misses home and so he says good-bye to the wild things and sails back home where he finds his supper waiting for him.

STARTERS

Materials Needed:
1. A box with a hole cut in the lid big enough for a hand, puppet decorating materials – yarn, laces, pipe cleaners, fabric scraps, large buttons, beads, ribbons.

2. Egg cartons in assorted colors, sheet of paper, scissors.

Procedure:
1. Place the decorating material inside the box. Have children take turns pulling something from the box and telling what they could make with it.

2. Count the egg cups in a carton. Cover half the cups with the piece of paper and count the uncovered cups. Cover eight of the cups and count the uncovered cups. Cut each carton into three groups of four cups.

EXTENDERS

Materials Needed:
1. Book.

2. Paper and crayons, gold foil (for moon), scissors, glue, clear plastic wrap, tape.

3. Four section egg cups cut in #2 above, scissors, glue, tape, staplers, decorating material from #1 above.

4. Classroom chairs.

Procedure:
1. Turn through the illustrations again and note how the illustration grow in size and, then after the rumpus, diminish in size.

   Draw attention to the cross hatchings (lines) in Sendak's style of illustrating.

   Compare the first view of Max's room to the view on the last page.

2. Draw a picture of a forest at night. Cut a moon from the gold foil and glue to your picture. Cover the picture with plastic wrap. Tape the ends to the reverse side.

3. Use the four section egg cartons to make "wild thing" puppets. Punch two finger holes on the hinged side of the puppet for manipulating the mouth. Decorate the puppet.

4. Use chairs to make Max's boat. Climb into the boat. Give directions for the following pretend activities: Paddle the boat to where the wild things are. Climb out of the boat. Place a crown on your head (use crown pattern found on page 162 or 163) and let the rumpus begin! STOP! Climb back into the boat. Paddle home. Climb out of the boat. Go into your room and eat your supper.

Biography

Jean Stangl has over thirty years experience in the Early Childhood field both as a classroom teacher and as a Community College and University instructor. Seven years ago she found a new way to share her experiences with children and teachers – she became an author! Jean is the author of over 200 magazine items and 20 books. A good number of her books are books for the classroom and teacher resource books. Her ideas and projects have been tested in the classroom and with her grandchildren, one of whom inspired her to write her first book. Jean has three grown sons and three grandchildren and lives with her husband in Camarillo, California. She travels a great deal and continues to teach educational classes and present seminars.